Teach Your Child to Learn

A Parent's Guide

Simple and Tested Techniques That Work

Author: Jan Sixt

Jan Sixt's Teach To Learn Press
Avon Lake, OH

D1520560

Teach Your Child to Learn, A Parent's Guide:
Simple and Tested Techniques That Work

For further information, contact the publisher: Jan Sixt's Teach To Learn Press, www.jstutor.com.

The author has made every diligent effort to ensure that the information in this book is complete and accurate. She assumes no responsibility for errors or omissions that are inadvertent or inaccurate, and makes no warranties or representations of any kind concerning the techniques and other information contained in this book. No guarantee is made that the author's methods will improve any particular individual. The views and opinions expressed in the book are not intended to endorse any product, procedure, or person.

Library of Congress Control Number: 2012900064

ISBN: 978-0-9849361-0-6

Dedicated to my students past, present, and future.
You will never know how much you helped me grow.

Especially dedicated to my own children, John and Kate.
If you don't know them, you've missed the best part of me.

What Others Say

Jan Sixt has a deep breadth of understanding regarding curricular matters. What makes her unique is that she can teach these curricular areas with efficacy to students of all ages. She is aware of student expectations and assessments and prepares students for these as well.

—David Lovering, Principal at Willow Ridge Elementary,
Amherst, New York.

I have seen Jan Sixt be really effective with a child who was struggling in high school. A child who wanted to be successful, just lost the ability to do it, and didn't know how to get it back. Now, years later, as I review Jan's techniques in this book, I see the strategies that our daughter is still using to be successful at the college level. Thank you, Jan.

—Greg Palmer, Parent, Member Avon Lake School Board,
RN, CMPE, FACHE, FHFMA, CPHQ, CPC.

Teach Your Child to Learn has a strong message and is a gift that can help other kids learn. Jan Sixt gave my daughter a new outlook on learning.

—Mary Campisi, Parent, Author of romance and women's fiction,
(www.marycampisi.com)

Table of Contents

Acknowledgements

With grateful recognition for their heartening support, their motivating interest, and their savvy expertise, I thank:

My children, Kate and John
My daughter-in-law, Thuy
My son-in-law, Anthony
Sheldon Harper (harperlee80@wowway.com)
Shelley Hussey (www.shelleyhussey.com; www.shelleyhussey.net)
Fred Luthy
Jane Dash
Mary Campisi (www.marycampisi.com)
Onkham Rattanaphasouk
Carolynn Cheatham
Rex Harper
Debra Rohde (www.rohdemd.com)

How to Use This Book

From the parent's point of view:

I have very little time. I'm torn. I have so many things to do, but I want to help my child learn. What's the answer? I'm a parent, not a teacher. It seems as though things have changed so much since I was in school. I'm lost, and it's so hard to watch my child struggle.

From the child's point of view:

Hey, I'm a kid. I *want* to get better grades. I don't want to make my teacher and my parents mad at me, but I just don't understand this stuff. Everybody else gets it except me. If I could do my homework, then my mom and dad would be proud of me, but school is so hard. I try. Really, I do!

From my point of view:

I'm a private tutor. I can show you how to apply the practical techniques I've developed over four decades of working with students like your child. I know your life is very, very busy. I was in your shoes not so long ago, juggling work, family responsibilities, and the needs of my own two growing children. Let me show you how to better use the time you *can* spend to help your child with homework.

This book is organized by subject. Each chapter describes techniques, starting with an essential one, to help the student "get it" and to smooth the road to learning. Over the years the gender of my students has been about 50-50, so I'll use both male and female pronouns in this book.

One of the closing chapters explains organizational and study skills for test-taking and time management. As a parent you'll discover simple ways to capture your child's natural curiosity and readiness to learn.

I know these techniques work, so let's get started.

Chapter One

Spelling/Phonics

IF I COULD KNOW ONLY ONE THING ABOUT *SPELLING*, IT WOULD BE . . . *PHONICS*.

Why? Because letters represent speech sounds. Those who speak English can use phonics to learn how to read and to write. Imagine your child knowing how to match letters and letter combinations with their sounds, instead of memorizing all of the letters in a word, or having to write each word ten times.

SPELLING AND PHONICS:

First, I want to share what I have found to be the most useful elements of phonics. We'll look at the basic tools of phonics and how to use them. Then we'll get to the exceptions.

CONSONANTS

b	box	p	pie
c	cat (hard "k" sound) city (soft "s" sound)	q	queen ("kwee" sound) quiche ("kee" sound)
d	dot	r	rabbit
f	five	s	sun
g	goat (hard "g" sound) giraffe (soft "j" sound)	t	turtle
h	happy	v	van
j	jump	w	water
k	kite	x	x-ray
l	little	y	yellow
m	man	z	zipper
n	nut		

Figure 1.1

11

BLENDS: Letter combinations that make a blended sound.

bl	black	**sn**	snow
br	brown	**sp**	spider
ch	cheese	**spl**	splash
cl	clock	**spr**	spring
cr	cry	**squ**	square
dr	draw	**st**	stop
fl	fly	**str**	straw
fr	frog	**sw**	sweater
gl	glue	**th**	they
gr	green	**thr**	throw
pl	play	**tr**	train
pr	present	**tw**	twig
qu	quite	**wh**	white
sc	scary		
sk	ski		
scr	scribble		**Silent Letter Blends**
sh	shut	**gn**	**gn**at ("g" is silent../nat)
shr	shrimp	**kn**	**kn**ot ("k" is silent../not)
sl	sled	**wr**	**wr**ap ("w" is silent../rap)
sm	small	**ps**	**Ps**alm ("p" is silent../salm)

Figure 1.2

VOWELS: *a, e, i, o, u,* and sometimes *y.*

	Short Vowels		"R" Controlled Vowels	
a	cat	"ar"	car	
e	men	"or"	horn	
i	pig	"er"	locker	
o	hot	"ir"	girl	
u	nut	"ur"	church	
	Long Vowels		**Sometimes "y"**	
a	cake			
e	street	y	my, by—(sound of long *i*)	
i	ice	y	busy—(sound of long *e*)	
o	open	y; y	mystery—(short *i* and long *e*)	
u	cube	y; y	mystify—(short *i* and long *i*)	

Figure 1.3

Short vowel sounds are usually in words having only one vowel, as these do: *bat, egg, sit, pot,* and *stump.*

They also often occur in words with only one vowel per syllable. For example, the two syllables in *seven* (sev-en), *singing* (sing-ing), and *jacket* (jack-et) all contain short vowels in both syllables.

Long vowel sounds usually occur in words having two vowels per word or per syllable. For example, the words *bake, goat,* and *maintain* (main-tain) have long vowel sounds.

A long vowel sound can be spelled with two vowels next to each other, such as in the word *goat*; or with a vowel-consonant-*e*, such as in the word *bake*. In both cases, the first vowel is sounded, but the second vowel . . . the *a* in *goat* or the final *e* in *bake* . . . make no sound at all. In other words, the second vowels remain "silent."

The **"R"** controlled vowels commonly appear in many English words. The sound of the vowels (*ar, er, ir, or, ur*) are distinctive when the vowel is followed by an *r*. (Figure 1.3) Interestingly, the *er* (me**r**chant), *ir* (shi**r**t), and *ur* (t**ur**n) all make the same sound. The *ar* (b**ar**n) and *or* (c**or**n) each make their own individual sound.

13

Sometimes the letter *y* is used as a vowel. It typically mimics the long *e* (dizzy), long *i* (style), or short *i* (mystic).

ODDBALLS: Common—but weird!—vowel combinations.
These exceptions have most often tripped my students.

au	Paul, auto	
ew	new, flew	
oo	look, book	(Both pairs of words are spelled with *oo* but
oo	cool, stool	they make different sounds.)
oi	oil, soil	(Both pairs of words are spelled differently, but
oy	toy, boy	the *oi* and *oy* sound the same.)
ou	ouch, cloud	(Both pairs of words are spelled differently, but
ow	cow, flower	the *ou* and *ow* sound the same.)
ow	snow, flow	(Has long *o* sound.)

Figure 1.4

When your child understands the information above, he will be well-prepared for a typical elementary school spelling list test. Maybe, just maybe, he'll remember to think about letter sounds and combinations when he's writing, too!

As your child advances into the intermediate and middle school levels, he should understand prefixes and suffixes. The list below is not a complete one, but mastering it will provide a better grasp of other such additions to the beginnings and endings of word roots.

PREFIXES:

ante	before	antebellum
anti	against	antibiotic
auto	self	automobile
bene	good	beneficial
circum	around	circumnavigate
de	away from, down	deforest
demi, hemi, semi	half	demigod, hemisphere semicircular
dis	not, opposite	dismount
equi	equal	equilateral

14

extra	beyond	**extra**ordinary
geo	earth	**geo**graphy
homo	same, like	**homo**graph
hyper	too much, over	**hyper**active
hypo	too little, under	**hypo**dermic
il, im, in, ir	not, in, on	**il**legal, **im**mature, **in**terrupt, **ir**regular
mal	badly, not enough	**mal**adjusted
mega	large	**mega**lopolis
micro	small	**micro**chip
mono	one	**mono**tone
non	not	**non**sense
over	too much	**over**protective
poly	many	**poly**nomial
post	after	**post**pone
pre	before	**pre**view
re	again, back	**re**open
sub	less than, below	**sub**marine
super	greater than	**super**market
tele	far	**tele**phone
trans	across	**trans**port
un	not, opposite	**un**real

SUFFIXES:

able, ible	capable	move**able**, convert**ible**
age	state of	teen**age**
al	of, like	minim**al**
an, ian	one who belongs to	Americ**an**, Ital**ian**
ant, ate	one who	contest**ant**, candid**ate**
cious	quality of	deli**cious**
dom	state	king**dom**
en	made of	hard**en**
er, or	one who	bak**er**, doct**or**
ful	full of	wonder**ful**
hood	state of	child**hood**
ish	like, similar	redd**ish**
ist	one who does	chem**ist**
ity, ty	having character of	clar**ity**, loyal**ty**
ize	cause to do	real**ize**
less	without	life**less**

15

ly	quality of, similar	lovely
ment, ness	state of	enjoyment, kindness
ous	full of	generous
ship	state of, having skill	censorship
some	full of	wholesome
tude	quality	gratitude
ward	in the direction	northward
y	full of, like	rainy

Figure 1.5

THE TECHNIQUE

Now that we have the technical tools in hand, let's get to the techniques that will help your kiddos succeed in *spelling*!

When your child uses the sounds that the letters are making (Figure 1.6), instead of memorizing the order of the letters, spelling will become much easier.

The Spelling Organizer

List Word	Blends	Long Vowels	Short Vowels	"R" Controlled Vowels	Silent Letters	Prefixes and Suffixes	Odd-Balls Exceptions
splash	splash		splash				
dragons	dragons		dragons			dragons	
normal			normal	normal			
fourth	fourth						fourth
believe		believe			believe		believe
reopen		reopen	reopen			reopen	
slight	slight	slight			slight		

Figure 1.6

- Each spelling word has its own row on the chart.

- After pronouncing the spelling word, your child should analyze it to see if it contains blends, prefixes, or suffixes.

16

- Next, the word's vowels should be classified as long, short, *r* controlled, or silent; remembering that some consonants can also be silent.

- If parts of the spelling word don't fit easily into any of the list's columns, that spelling word is banished to the exception, or *oddball,* category. This word now deserves special attention because your child will not be able to *hear* the sounds as he has become accustomed.

This approach has made learning to spell organized and effective. This is an example of organized thinking. After a few weeks of using this method, your child will be able to handle his studying by himself! The added bonus . . . spelling is improved whenever your child writes. That means improved spelling on book reports, essay tests, even on those thank you notes to Grandma and Grandpa. Wonder of wonders!

Hi Jan,

We really appreciate your help with Jacob. I have noticed a big improvement in his letters and in his sounding out words.

Amy

Chapter Two

Grammar/Parts of Speech

IF I COULD KNOW ONLY ONE THING ABOUT *GRAMMAR*, IT WOULD BE . . . THE *PARTS OF SPEECH*.

Picture it: your daughter must use her spelling words in complete sentences. Your middle schooler must learn twenty vocabulary words, and you know six of them. Your high schooler must properly use the vocabulary from a novel he has been reading with his class. Your child has asked you to help him learn his social studies words . . . and tomorrow he has a science test with more vocabulary!

Twenty-six letters in the alphabet spell all of the printed English words. That includes all of the books in the library, in our school textbooks, and in our business world. Amazing! Just twenty-six letters!

Similarly, only nine parts of speech build our sentences. The nine are:

Article (Some sources do not include the article as a separate part of speech.)
Adjective
Noun
Pronoun
Verb
Adverb
Preposition
Conjunction
Interjection

The order in which the parts of speech are arranged give the written word meaning. For example, you understand the following words individually:

cream dog eat my likes ice to

However, their collective meaning is clear only when placed in proper order:

My dog likes to eat ice cream.

The parts of speech function in relationship to each other. Not all are used in every sentence, and there may be exceptions to these basic rules. However, most sentences have at least one noun or pronoun which functions as a subject, followed by a verb. (In most cases, <u>someone</u> or <u>something</u> / <u>does</u> or <u>is</u> something.)

Other examples:

> *The **baby** / **crawled** across the rug.*
> *The **flower** / **is** a daisy.*

Think of the parts of speech as members of a family. They have names and functions, as do the members of your family. Let's say that Mark, Angela, Bryan, and Olivia are members of the Smith family. We know their names but not their relationships to each other. In fact, each family member has many relationships:

Smith Family Members	Function
Mark:	husband, father, uncle, employee, son-in-law, etc.
Angela:	wife, mother, daughter, neighbor, sister-in-law, aunt, etc.
Bryan:	brother, hockey teammate, nephew, paperboy, etc.
Olivia:	daughter, sister, cousin, niece, pet owner, granddaughter, etc.

The people in my example have many functions. The ways they interact with each other depend upon whom they are associating with at the moment. Each person's identity is constant, but he acts differently as his associations vary.

Similarly, the parts of speech are individual members which function according to the other words around them. Some generalizations can be made about these nine members of the "parts of speech" family.

Article— Only three—**a, an, the.**
Special adjectives—usually come before nouns.
Sometimes called noun markers because nouns are located within a word or two of the article.
Ex: **a** dish
an elephant
the blue bathtub

Adjective— Usually comes before nouns.
Describes nouns or other adjectives.
Ex: **brown** bananas
soft, fuzzy sweater
respectable mayor

Noun— Names a: **person**—Pat
place—kitchen
thing—finger
idea—freedom
quality—beauty
Has four functions:
subject
direct object
indirect object
object of the preposition

Functions as *subject* if it *does* the action.

Ex: **Bob** gave Mother the letter in the kitchen.

- *Who did the action? Bob gave, making Bob the subject of this sentence.*

Functions as *direct object* if it *receives* the action.

Ex: Bob gave Mother the **letter** in the kitchen.

- *What receives the action? The letter was moved from Bob to his mother.*

Functions as **indirect object** if **indirectly receives** the action.

Ex: Bob gave **Mother** the letter in the kitchen.

- *Bob physically picked up the letter; he did not pick up and move Mother. However, his mother did indirectly receive the action.*

Functions as **object of a preposition** when ending the prepositional phrase.

Ex: Bob gave Mother the letter in the **kitchen**.
  • *The prepositional phrase in the kitchen begins with the preposition, "in", and ends with the object of the preposition, kitchen.*

Pronoun— Replaces nouns—**I, you, he, it, we, they, me, her, us, them,** etc. Has same functions as nouns:

Subject: He gave Mother the letter in the kitchen.

Direct object: Bob gave Mother **it** in the kitchen.

Indirect object: Bob gave **her** the letter in the kitchen.

Object of a preposition: Bob gave Mother the letter in **there**.

Verb— Shows action or movement (active voice): **run, play, eat, swim, blink,** etc.

Shows state of being (passive voice): **is, am, was, were, are,** etc.

Adverb— Describes the action (main job).
Describes other adverbs.
Describes adjectives.

Ex: She **quietly** tiptoed up the stairs.
Mrs. Woods **calmly** rescued her kitten from the tree.
I am **really** happy to know you.
Martin **very often** plays the guitar, **too**.

Preposition—Shows a position: **in, on, up, down, around, between, to, by,** etc.

Ex: She drove the car *down the street, around the corner*, and *into the garage.*

  • Prepositional phrases begin with the preposition and end with a noun or pronoun, which functions as the object of the preposition.

Conjunction—Joining words: **and, but, or, yet, while, because, if,** etc.

Ex: Joins two subjects:
Mary **and** Caleb painted the shed.

Joins two verbs:
Mary sings **or** dances every morning.

Joins two adverbs:
He tenderly **yet** firmly bandaged his leg wounds.

Joins two clauses:
I ordered spaghetti, **but** he chose pork chops.

Interjections— Shows surprise or emotion: **wow, golly, heck, aw, hey, alas, yea,** etc.
Usually at beginning or end of sentence.

Ex: **Ouch,** I burned myself.
Wow, this is fun!
The dog tipped his water bowl, **darn.**

THE TECHNIQUE

Now let's get to your daughter's homework assignment where she must use her spelling words in complete sentences or study that list of vocabulary words. Simply check the dictionary or the glossary, which is in the back of most textbooks, and note the part of speech. Think of a situation in which the word could be used. An easy way to do that is to incorporate part of the word's definition into your original sentence.

Let me give you an example. Let's say the vocabulary word is *myth*. A *myth* is a traditional or cultural story which tries to explain a particular custom, belief, or natural event like thunder or the change of the seasons. A myth is a noun.

Since *myth* is a noun, the word can function in four different ways: as a **subject, direct object, indirect object,** or as an **object of a preposition.** Now let's think of some situation that would involve a traditional story that explains a phenomenon or custom.

As a **subject:** *The myth told the story about the ancient culture's sun god.* Working the context clues *story* and *culture* into the sentence from the definition further helps the student understand the vocabulary word. This also makes a stronger sentence which teachers love to love.

As a **direct object:** *As the audience listened intently, Pete recited the **myth** at the medieval festival.*

As an **object of a preposition:** *In the **myth,** the sun god smiled at the people when they worshipped him.*

Here's another example. Let's take the word *expound*. *Expound* means to give a detailed explanation. *Expound* is a verb.

A verb shows action or movement, so think of some situation that would involve someone explaining something in detail.

As a **verb:** *The college professor **expounded** about Isaac Newton's three Laws of Motion.*

Here's still another example. Let's compare the words *well* and *good*. *Well* is an adverb; *good* is an adjective.

An adverb describes the action, or verb. An adjective describes a noun or pronoun.

As an **adverb:** She dances ***well.***
As an **adjective:** She is a **good** dancer.

Dear Jan,

Pat said the exam prep has been very helpful. I'm sad, and happy to say that Pat's last day with you will be Thursday.

Your guidance in (teaching my son) organizational skills and . . . tips in math and grammar has been invaluable. Thanks so much.

Sincerely,
Barbara

Chapter Three

Reading/Identify Your Purpose

IF I COULD KNOW ONLY ONE THING ABOUT *READING*, IT WOULD BE . . . *IDENTIFY YOUR PURPOSE* FOR READING.

Why bother to read? What is your goal? Are you reading for factual information or to broaden your awareness of life? Are you reading to find the numbers in a story problem so you can do the math calculations? Maybe you are reading purely for pleasure.

Although many aspects of reading are similar, I will talk here about fiction and nonfiction reading comprehension. (The math chapter, Chapter 6, has some helpful tips for reading and understanding word problems.)

FICTION
Elements of the Story

The **elements of the story** are basic to full understanding and appreciation of the narrative.

PLOT—significant action
CHARACTER—people, animals, etc
SETTING—time and place where story occurs
THEME—controlling idea or central insight
POINT OF VIEW—who actually tells the story

All of these elements intertwine, but each deserves individual attention.

PLOT

PLOT is the sequence of events of the story or the significant action in a central conflict, or problem. Conflict results from a clash of actions, ideas, or desires. The main character—the protagonist—is at odds with someone or something.

25

The protagonist is the main character who has the conflict or problem. The antagonist is the person or force against the main character. Simply stated, the protagonist has the problem which the antagonist has made. In the case of person versus (vs.) himself, the protagonist and the antagonist are both the same person. (This would be the classic illustration of a person spitting into the wind—duh!) Many stories read at school-age level are about the person against himself conflict.

The conflict usually fits into one of these categories:

1. **Person vs. Person**—The main character is pitted against another person or group, such as a bully on the playground.

2. **Person vs. Environment**—Here the main character is at odds with some external force, which could be:

   Physical—trapped in an elevator.

   Nature—caught in a blizzard.

   Society—being female prior to women's suffrage.

   Fate—winning the lottery and then being besieged by friends you never knew you had.

3. **Person vs. Himself**—Now the main character is fighting some element of his own making, which could be:

   Physical—a surgeon accidentally cuts off a finger while doing home carpentry.

   Mental—a teenager experiments with drugs and damages his brain.

   Emotional—a woman is jealous of a co-worker's skill and beauty.

   Moral—a person gets caught shoplifting.

At the beginning of the story during the exposition, the tone of the story is set and important background information is given. The reader is usually introduced to some of the characters and the setting of the story is established. At this point an inciting event occurs, and this causes conflict to the main character. In a series of rising and falling actions, the protagonist attempts to solve the conflict. If he is unsuccessful, more rising and falling actions occur. Sometimes the initial problem is solved. However, this may cause another subset of problems.

For example, let's say that the neighborhood bully is making trouble for main character, Pat, by teasing her (*rising action*). She ignores the bully, hoping to fix the problem (*falling action*). The bully heats up the action and begins to trip and shove Pat (*more rising action*). Finally, Pat tells the bully's parents about the harassment and the bully is punished. The event that leads to the solution of the problem is called the *climax* of the story. The story's *resolution* occurs when the conflict is resolved. At that point the story ends because the conflict has ended.

The plot of the story can be diagrammed. (See Figure 3.1)

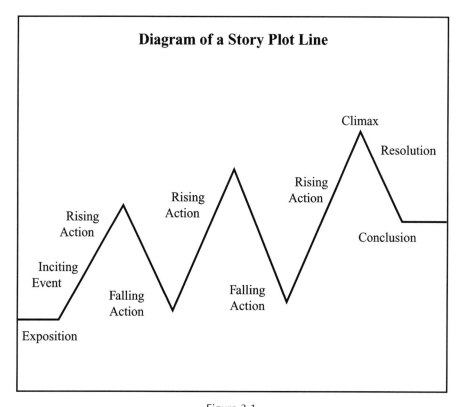

Figure 3.1

27

CHARACTER

CHARACTER is another element of the story. Understanding the central character helps the reader better understand real people. The author allows the reader to listen to what the main character and others say about each other. Furthermore, the reader can *observe* how the characters interact.

Behavior trumps words. This mimics real life, which is why reading fiction can be such a valuable tool for personal growth. A bonus to real life situations occurs when the author allows the reader to learn what the characters *think* and *feel*. In real life we know only our own thoughts and emotions. We continually have to guess at what real people are thinking—and most of the time we're wrong!

Since the character's behavior is more important than what is said, let me give you additional usable information. A character's behavior can remain constant throughout the story. I would consider Cinderella to be a *static* character, because she was the same sort of person at the beginning of the story as at the end. Undoubtedly, it took effort on her part to remain cheerful and kind in the face of her problems, but Cinderella really didn't change.

On the other hand, Scrooge in *A Christmas Carol* by Charles Dickens proved to be a *dynamic* character. He developed and fundamentally changed from a "bah, humbug" into a person who embraced the spirit of Christmas. For this change to be convincing, the author must allow his character to be able to make this change. We wouldn't expect a four-year old to be the star player of a professional basketball team. However, in my example it was certainly possible for Scrooge to change his attitude. The author gave his character the free will to make the decision to alter his views about the holiday. (On the contrary, in some stories the reader is encouraged to suspend this principle for the sake of the action. It is *not* credible to believe that a character can leap tall buildings in a single bound, or huff and puff to blow a house down. Those exceptions are viewed by the reader with a wink and a nod as the reader immerses into the fantasy.)

Additionally, a character must be *motivated* to make a change. Scrooge was encouraged to remember the fun of the Christmas holiday from years past. He was invited to celebrate with his family in the present. Finally, Scrooge was given a glimpse of his possible fate. This motivation was the key to Scrooge's personal development.

Finally, an author must allow his character sufficient time in order to make this change. We would be skeptical if a serial murderer, who had served one week of his sentence, claimed that he had found the Lord and was no longer a threat to society. In my example, it took a "thumping" from the ghosts of Christmas Past, Present, and Future, until Scrooge finally saw the value in changing his personal outlook.

THEME

THEME often explains the change that takes place in the character—why he solved his problem. Remember the conflict in the section about plot? Rather than state the theme, authors *show it,* giving the reader a greater understanding of life.

Titles can often reveal the theme. Some examples are *Kidnapped, A Tale of Two Cities, To Kill a Mockingbird, The Scarlet Letter,* or *Atlas Shrugged.* It might not surprise you that my favorite such title is *Teach Your Child to Learn, A Parent's Guide.* Consider the title when thinking about why an author bothered to write the book.

Theme should be stated in a complete sentence if your child needs to write about this element of the story. Theme should rely on the facts stated in the story. The most important details of the plot support the central idea. If your child can explain why the main character has solved the conflict, he will be able to pinpoint the story's theme.

POINT OF VIEW

POINT OF VIEW is an interesting story element which combines the *who* and the *how*: *who* tells the story and *how* much does that character actually know? Of course, the author controls these details revealing the character's thoughts and feelings. In real life, we continually judge the source of our infor-mation. Current political news events, changing scientific data, as well as ordinary family dynamics can be confusing when information is exchanged from differing points of view.

There is a fable told in India about six blind men from the Brahmaputra River Valley, who describe an elephant from each of their points of view. One of the men touches the elephant's side and says it's a wall. Another touches the trunk and calls it a snake. A third man thinks the tail makes the animal a rope. A fourth blind man identifies the sharp tusk as a spear, while the man who touched an ear thought it to be a fan. The last of the group of six felt a leg and proclaimed it a tree. Wall, snake, rope, spear, fan, tree . . . each was an honest judgment from a blind man's point of view.

Who tells the story and how much does that character really know? Mix in deception, trickery, and other negatives, including outright lying, and the reader gets some dicey practice for understanding real life!

Point of view can be divided into the following categories:

Omniscience—The story is told by the author, who knows everything— his only prerogative since he created the story. Omniscience has the largest scope because the author not only tells the reader what the characters say, feel, and think, but reveals why they behave as they do.

Limited Omniscience—The story is told via a third person, or by one character in the story. That one character explains the events, but this reasoning is filtered through this character's knowledge and bias.

First Person—Again one character tells the story. This style is recognizable because this particular character refers to himself as "I" or "me" throughout the story. First person point of view filters the events through this character's knowledge and bias.

Objective Point of View—The author simply records what is seen and heard without interpretation or comment. Nothing is explained, so the reader is a spectator, in much the same way as he would be when "people watching" at the mall or park. Objective point of view mimics real life.

SETTING

SETTING is the final story element. It establishes the story in a particular place at a particular time. Perhaps the story takes place in Virginia during the Civil War, or in the Atlantic Ocean as the *Titanic* sinks. These settings can easily be identified.

However, many stories don't give the reader a clear place and date. Perhaps the story takes place in Aunt Helen's kitchen, but the reader must infer this because the main character is involved with measuring ingredients, mixing, and cooking. The reader infers that it is late summer during the 1700s because Auntie is canning tomatoes from her garden on a fireplace hearth. She is hurrying to finish before the last rays of sunshine fade into night. Using context clues like these can be extremely helpful as the reader pieces together the story's "puzzle."

THE TECHNIQUE

As your child reads, she will have a better understanding if she reads with a purpose. That goal may be to answer comprehension questions, write a summary, give an oral book report, or pass a test. Sometimes a teacher will assign the report or worksheet after the class has read the material. In this case, most students will have to reread the book as they search for their answers. I think this approach wastes a lot of valuable time and frustrates the student because it forces the student to do the reading twice.

Since the story elements are basic, using them can help your child perform better and faster. To accomplish this goal, have your child list the story elements on a sheet of paper. Use this list as a guide:

Level One—Moderately Experienced Reader

Plot
    Conflict—What is the problem?
              What type of problem is it?
                    Person vs. Person
                    Person vs. Environment
                    Person vs. Himself

    Resolution— How was the problem solved?

Character
    Protagonist—Who was the character who had the problem?
    Antagonist—Who made the problem?

Theme
    Why was the problem solved?
    Did the main character have to change in order to solve the problem?

Point of View
    Which one of the characters told the story? Perhaps the author or a narrator told the story.

Setting
When and where did the story take place?

Level Two—More Experienced Reader

Plot
Conflict
Inciting Event
Rising Action
Falling Action
Climax
Resolution

Character
Protagonist
Antagonist
Other supporting characters?
Any dynamic or static characters?
What motivated the characters to behave as they did?

Theme

Point of View

Setting

For the preschool level listener or beginner reader, use the following list when discussing the story. You will get a good idea of how well your child understood what you just read to her or, more importantly, what she just read to you!

Who: Who was in the story?
Where: Where was that character?
What: What was that person's problem? What did that person do?
When: When did that happen?
Why: Why did that happen?
How: How did that happen?

A skillful author weaves the elements of the story into his creation piece by piece, allowing the reader to discover the whole work as one would assemble a puzzle. Sometimes it is not possible to identify each element until the student has read the complete book. For that reason, have your child think about each category on the above list periodically (for example, after each chapter). When your child finds a detail that he would like to include, have him record the book's page number on his note sheet along with the entry. He will not have to search for that point later if he would like to cite it in his book report. Many teachers require quoted material from the story's text in order to substantiate a student's assertions.

When a reader begins reading a story, it's like watching a movie. For a few minutes the reader, or viewer, is confused until the relationship between the characters becomes clear. Have your child use a single sheet of paper for each character who is introduced in the story. Then he should write down what he learns about each character when the author gives some new tidbit or detail. For example: the character's description, age, relationship to other characters, personality traits, etc. Be sure to include the page number next to the note for easy reference in case your child needs to review the detail and cite it in his homework.

NONFICTION
Note-Taking Skills

Note-taking skills are basic to understanding nonfiction.

Nonfiction reading includes social studies, general science, health, biology, chemistry, geography, economics—those heavy-hitting core subjects that span the entire school experience. These fact-laden studies get increasingly more complex and lengthy year by year. Most of your child's homework will be generated from nonfiction subjects: worksheets, study guides, questions to answer after reading the chapter, and finally, studying for the dreaded quizzes and tests. As a parent, it isn't necessary that you explain the significance of the Magna Carta or the difference between mitosis and meiosis. No one is hindering you if you would like to discuss these topics with your child, but my point is to empower your child with the note-taking skills that will help make the subject matter clear to him via his own efforts.

Again, the act of reading needs a purpose. Nonfiction reading results in test-taking questions involving true/false, multiple-choice, matching, and fill in the blanks, in addition to short answers and essay type responses. Textbooks give facts, as well as explanations and reasons. These books are organized into units, chapters, headings, and subheadings—a great help with note-taking.

NOTE-TAKING

People communicate with each other in complete sentences. If I said the word "orange" to you, you could not be sure if I was referring to the fruit or the color. Maybe I meant Halloween. As you can see, I really didn't communicate with you. In order to make you understand my message, I would need to give you the complete sentence. "My favorite color is orange." Now we've communicated!

However, if you needed to remember that piece of information, perhaps for a test at some future date, you would not store it in your memory as a complete sentence. Your brain doesn't need that many words. I've realized that students do better when they read the complete sentences, reword the information according to their personal understanding, and condense the meaning into a note. Those are the steps which work:

Read............Understand............Reword............Note

Let's look at them each individually. First of all, what information is noteworthy? Here's my short list:

		Example
Factual Information:	Who	George Washington
	What	fought in American Revolution
	Where	colonies
	When	1776
Explanations:	Why	free colonies from British rule
	How	helped by patriots
	Reasons	high taxation/no representation
	Cause and Effect	birth of USA
	Conditional Ideas	if war lost . . . still belong to England

THE TECHNIQUE

So you're looking for the facts, reasons, conditional ideas, and cause and effect information, but how do you actually *take the notes*? Most students write down too much information. They want to copy the book's wording. However, that is not the most effective method. It's too robotic. The exercise of rewording forms synapses in the brain which promote memory. I want my students to engage in the process. They must really think about what they just read, so they can formulate their own way of saying it. In other words, people communicate with each other in complete sentences, but we don't *think* that way.

In fact, the brain stores memories as:

> *Relationships*—opposites: up/down, sweet/sour
> *Associations*—red traffic light: stop
> *Categories*—clothing items: pants, socks, shirt, belt
> *Symbols*—%, $, =, +
> *Abbreviations*—Mr., Rev., USA
> *Short phrases/grouping*—first president, Allied Powers, WWII
> *Pictures*

The point is to take the notes as clearly and as simply as possible so that your child retains the meaning of what he needs to remember. This is a skill that improves with practice. Your child will know if he's doing it correctly when he can answer the questions, complete the worksheets, or write the report without rereading the textbook. His notes become even more valuable when he has to study for those unit tests. He will be happily surprised to see how helpful his own personal notes will be when studying for semester exams. All the information from those chapters covered way back in September will come alive to him again when he rereads the notes that he made from his own understanding. Happy note-taking!

In the past while reading a book, I found myself thinking about everything else except the story. I could never stay focused for long enough to comprehend the main idea. Ms. Sixt taught me not only to take notes while reading, but also to ask myself questions about the story elements, like plot or theme. As I read, I began to interpret the point of the story and to anticipate what might happen next. Learning to predict outcomes enhanced my curiosity which made reading interactive and exciting. Understanding these concepts helped me improve my comprehension.

Sean

Chapter Four

Science/Social Studies

IF I COULD KNOW ONLY ONE THING ABOUT *SCIENCE AND SOCIAL STUDIES,* IT WOULD BE. . . *FLASHCARD/NOTE-TAKING.*

Science and social studies include biology, chemistry, psychology, health, geography, economics, history, religion, and government. They are heavy reading subjects. Their vocabulary includes terms like *cell division, osmosis, electron, isthmus, corporate bond, fascism, or constitutional monarchy—* words your child must know in order to understand the subject.

Many of the tests your child will take require what I call "regurgitation." He'll have to "give back" the various facts which he has learned on a test containing matching, true/false, multiple choice, and fill-in-the-blank type questions. Many tests are electronically scanned, largely preventing short essay questions/responses. Such a format lends itself to the fact-gathering which was basic to the note-taking in the reading chapter about nonfiction (Chapter 3).

THE TECHNIQUE

A flashcard technique I developed years ago has helped hundreds of students and they have given me a lot of positive feedback. I call it "note-taking on steroids," because a baby flashcard pairs with the regular one to more firmly and quickly meet the goal of note-taking: to express the most important facts in the simplest way while retaining the meaning. Here's how it works:

Let's start with the vocabulary term *monotheism.* Write that word on one side of a card or piece of paper (1.5" × 2" or so). On the other side write a short definition, somewhat like a crossword puzzle clue that suggest it but isn't definitive. Encourage your child to choose his own familiar words for this "trigger" function, because his ability to learn and remember the facts he's about to write begins with his own thinking process. Then, on a smaller card or piece of paper (the "baby" flashcard), repeat the word *monotheism* and leave the smaller card blank on the other side. Remind your child to stay focused on the exercise; distractions can dilute the concentration that's necessary.

Here are some examples. Remember, the words on side two of the regular flashcard should be your child's, not necessarily the ones I've used:

Example 1:

Flashcard Side One

Monotheism

Flashcard Side Two

**Belief—1 God
Judaism/Islam
Christianity**

Baby Flashcard (one side only)

Monotheism

Example 2:

Flashcard Side One

Polytheism

Flashcard Side Two

**Worship many
gods
Ancient Greece**

Baby Flashcard (one side only)

Polytheism

Example 3:

Flashcard Side One

Bill of Rights

Flashcard Side Two

First 10 amendments of U.S Constitution

Baby Flashcard (one side only)

Bill of Rights

Example 4:

The above are examples of useful flashcard combinations. Here is an example of a flashcard which is too obvious to be helpful:

Flashcard Side One

Marxism

Flashcard Side Two

Practice of philosophy of Karl Marx

Remember to select words that relate to your vocabulary term without using the side one word in the definition itself.

Now comes the fun part—a game that makes this process different from and more effective than simple "flash-carding". Put the three flashcards in a row, top to bottom, each with its side-two up. Then, mix the baby flashcards word-side up and begin matching the baby cards to the correct large flashcard. (Place the "babies" next to, not on top of, the large cards to make the turning of the cards faster.) Have your child place only the ones that he really knows. (No guessing at this point. If he guesses, he will only have to break the association before he learns the correct one. If he misses a few, that's part of the learning process. Guessing should be saved as a strategy, if all else fails, when actually taking the test. During the study time, *learning* is the goal.)

The challenge is to match the "baby" card with its larger card, which is then turned over to show the match—or not. When the two cards agree, your child will feel the rush of achievement. Success is a spur to keep at it. The matched cards can be set aside to be reviewed later, and your child can study the cards he hasn't yet mastered. In a few minutes, he'll be ready to repeat the process.

After the study session, place the paired cards he knows into a small container labeled LEARNED. (A zipper-locked sandwich bag will do nicely.) Put the other cards into a WORK-IN-PROGRESS bag. This conveniently separates and "files" the work.

If some combinations from the LEARNED bag get a bit fuzzy, your child can switch them to the WORK-IN-PROGRESS bag for further review. The goal, of course, is to empty the latter bag.

Understanding and using vocabulary is the core ingredient to learning most subjects. Encourage your child to think of other ways in which he can use the "flashcard-with-baby-flashcard" technique. (One of my students used pink and blue paper when making his flashcards for Spanish to help him learn the feminine and masculine nouns.)

Studying for me used to be very hard. I am a smart student, but like most teenagers in high school, I need to study to get a good grade and to know the material. After being taught the right study techniques, my grades improved a lot. The best part about (knowing the study techniques) is that I can (apply) them at home without a tutor.

The baby flashcards saved my biology grade because they helped me to understand the vocabulary words better. Another technique I use is taking notes on the worksheets that my classroom teachers give me. When I take my own notes, I understand the subject in my own way. The best thing about all of these techniques is that I can use them in almost every subject I have. They are unique and fit the way I learn best. I am going to use these studying tips throughout the rest of my high school and college years.

Leanne

Chapter Five

Writing/Sentence Structure

IF I COULD KNOW ONLY ONE THING ABOUT *WRITING,* IT WOULD BE . . . *SENTENCE STRUCTURE.*

When you talk, do people understand you? When you listen to others, do you understand them? These are the questions I ask my students when I teach writing and reading.

When you write, you *talk* to someone who isn't physically with you. The thank you note to Grandma and Grandpa, the letter to Mom and Dad when you're at summer camp, the letter that tells the plastics company your new toy was broken when you opened the box, the cover letter you attach to your resume— all are examples of writing that speaks.

Similarly, reading is *listening* to someone who isn't physically with you. Grandma, Mom and Dad, the customer service agent at the plastics company, the college's admissions officer are all listening to you speak as they read what you've written.

When writing, you get only one chance to effectively communicate with others. You cannot assess their body language or their facial expressions, which might give you a clue that you have confused them. You are not present to have a "do over" moment.

Happily, when you write, you have several tools that help you meet your need to be understood. The pivotal one is the proper use of sentence structure, and how to build each of three sentence types: *simple, compound,* and *complex.*

First, let's go back to the grammar chapter's parts of speech to refresh your memory about the function of the noun/pronoun and the verb. A complete sentence needs both—the noun or pronoun (functioning as a *subject*) and a verb (sometimes called a *predicate*). There are certain exceptions to needing a designated subject but, for the sake of clarity, I will talk to you about the normal sentence. Remember, the purpose of this book is to share the tutoring techniques which provide the most effective and immediate help, without getting tangled in the exceptions. If your child masters writing these three sentence types, he can take command of most classwork.

Sentences are constructed using clauses, which contain a subject/verb grouping. You can think of the clauses as the raw materials of sentence construction. There are two kinds of clauses, *independent* and *dependent* (sometimes called *subordinate*). The subject/verb combination is usually written with the subject preceding the verb. Here are some examples:

INDEPENDENT CLAUSE:

The **dog chewed** the bone.

Dog is the subject of this clause. **Chewed** is the verb.

The independent clause has a subject/verb combination and the clause makes sense. (If an independent clause is used alone, a complete sentence is formed.)

DEPENDENT CLAUSE:

After the **dog chewed** the bone.

Dog is still the subject of this clause; **chewed** is still the verb.

The dependent clause has a subject/verb combination, but the clause does not make sense on its own. If a dependent clause is used alone, only a partial sentence is formed. This construction is awkward and incomplete.

When your child writes complete sentences, he should place a subject/verb combination preferably near the beginning of the clause. The order in which the parts of speech are arranged gives the written word its meaning. When your child places the subject next to, and in front of the verb, he has followed a basic speech pattern of the English language. Furthermore, the clause must make sense (independent clause). If the clause has the subject/verb combination, but does not make sense on its own (dependent clause), it must be attached to an independent clause which enhances the meaning of both of the clauses.

Now let's use what we've learned.

SIMPLE SENTENCE STRUCTURE

The simple sentence uses one independent clause. It's used to answer factual questions that usually begin with the words *who, what, where,* **and** *when.*

Examples of Simple Sentence Structure

The **dog chewed** the bone.
• One subject, **dog,** followed by one verb.

Joey and **I ran** all the way home.
• Two subjects, **Joey** and **I,** share one verb.

Bob, Mark, Larry, and **Fred are** teammates.
• Several subjects, **Bob, Mark, Larry,** and **Fred,** share one verb.

We **ate** hot pizza from the box and **drank** soda from the can.
• One subject, **we,** shares two verbs.

We **bit, chewed,** and **swallowed** the pizza.
• A comma never separates the two verbs unless the verbs are part of a series of three or more verbs.
• One subject, **we,** shares three verbs.

A simple sentence needs to have at least one subject/verb combination.

Here are some typical questions which could be effectively answered using simple sentence structure:

Who is the main character in the story?
Nelson, the black Labrador retriever, is the story's main character.

What are the ingredients in your fruit salad?
Blueberries, strawberries, and blackberries are mixed together to make this fruit salad.

Where will you go after school?
The bus will drive us to the wrestling match in Fairmont, West Virginia.

When do you see your cousins?
I visit my cousins every summer.

COMPOUND SENTENCE STRUCTURE

The compound sentence uses two independent clauses that are joined by a coordinating conjunction (normally: *and, but, yet, or, nor,* semicolon *;*). The compound sentence is used to *compare* and *contrast* ideas. It can efficiently give two similar facts or two contrasting facts.

Examples of Compound Sentence Structure

Ally <u>likes</u> blue, *but* **Kate** <u>prefers</u> yellow.
• Two independent clauses joined with the coordinating conjunction, *but.*

George Washington <u>was</u> the first US president, *and* **he** <u>lived</u> at Mt. Vernon.
• Two independent clauses joined with the coordinating conjunction, *and.*

You can play soccer tonight, *or* **you can go** to the air show with your friends.
• Two independent clauses joined with the coordinating conjunction, *or.*
• A comma is needed before the conjunction in order to separate both independent clauses. No comma is required between the clauses if the semicolon is used in place of the conjunction.

A compound sentence needs to have at least one subject/verb combination in each of two independent clauses which are joined with a coordinating conjunction.

Here are some questions which could be answered with compound sentence structure:

Who is the *protagonist* and *antagonist* in this story selection?
Little Red Riding Hood was the protagonist, and the big bad wolf was the antagonist in this fairytale.

Where and *when* was the first airplane flown?
The first airplane flew from Kitty Hawk, North Carolina; it was 1903.

Compare the properties of the *equilateral* and *isosceles triangles.*
The equilateral triangle has three equal sides, but the isosceles triangle has only two equal sides.

COMPLEX SENTENCE STRUCTURE

The complex sentence uses one independent clause and one dependent clause that are joined by a subordinating conjunction (normally: *because, since, if, as, while, that, where, why, how, although, before, after, who, when, until*). The dependent clause begins with the subordinating conjunction followed by the subject/verb combination for that dependent clause. The complex sentence answers the questions *why* and *how*. The complex sentence *explains, gives reasons, expresses cause and effect*, or *conditional ideas*.

Examples of Complex Sentence Structure

Our **family** <u>watches</u> television *after* **we** <u>eat</u> dinner.
  • One independent clause followed by one dependent clause that starts with the subordinating conjunction, ***after***.

I <u>moved</u> back to Chicago *because* my **grandparents** <u>live</u> there.
  • One independent clause followed by one dependent clause beginning with the subordinating conjunction, ***because***.

If **John** <u>cleans</u> the garage, **he** <u>will</u> <u>get</u> his allowance.
  • One dependent clause beginning with the subordinate conjunction, ***if***, followed by an independent clause. When the dependent clause precedes the independent clause, a comma is used to separate the two clauses.

John <u>***will***</u> <u>***get***</u> *his allowance if* ***he*** <u>***cleans***</u> *the garage.*
  • The independent and dependent clauses have been reversed from the previous sentence. Flipping the clauses adds variety to your writing.

A complex sentence needs to have at least one subject/verb combination in both the independent clause and the dependent clause which are joined by a subordinating conjunction.

Here are some examples of inquiries where complex sentence structure could be used:

Why did the thirteen colonies want to break away from British rule?
  The thirteen colonies wanted to break away from the mother country because Britain taxed its colonies too heavily.

47

How does a virus embed itself into a healthy cell?
When a virus contacts a healthy cell, it embeds its genes into the DNA of the cell.

Explain the cause of lightning.
As the rising air of a cloud pushes against dirt and ice within the cloud, static electricity builds.

How does sunlight affect photosynthesis?
Green plants, which contain chlorophyll, are able to use the energy from sunlight to convert water and carbon dioxide into sugar.

HONORABLE MENTIONS
Other Important Skills

What to Say

A well-constructed sentence is a pivot point for the writing skill. Knowing how to write simple, compound, and complex sentences will really help your child academically. Now that he knows how to *say it,* the next question is what to *write about.*

Let's say your child is writing a book report about a fictional story. He will please his teacher very much if he discusses the story using its literary elements. (See Reading, Chapter 3 for an in-depth discussion of the story elements.)

Basic:

Plot
 Conflict
 Resolution

Character
 Protagonist
 Antagonist

Theme
Point of View
Setting

Expanded Basic with More Detail:

Plot
    Conflict
    Inciting Event
    Rising Action
    Falling Action
    Climax
    Resolution

Character
    Protagonist
    Antagonist
    Other supporting characters?
    Any dynamic or static characters?
    What motivated the characters to behave as they did?

Theme
Point of View
Setting

Expanded Basic, Including Other Subsets of the Elements:

Use all of the above with attention to other subsets of the elements: drama, suspense, dilemma, stock characters, tone, symbolism, dialog, irony, etc.— there's a million of 'em!

....

If your child is writing about something in the nonfiction area, he should think about note-taking as described in the chapter on reading: the *who, what, where, when, why, how, explanations, cause and effect, reasons*, and *conditional ideas*. Your child could discuss all of these which apply to the article he is summarizing.

Whether writing fiction or nonfiction, make sure that your child takes notes in the above categories so he can organize his thinking. Then he can select the best notes, organize his thoughts, and write simple, compound, and complex sentences to express himself clearly.

Learning to transition from one thought to another and from one paragraph to the next smooths your child's writing. Here is a list of some transitional words that will help him do just that. Keep the list handy for reference.

Contrast Words:

in contrast
although
on the contrary
even though
on the other hand
conversely
but
however

Cause and Effect Words:

consequently
thus
as a result
since
because
therefore
accordingly

Support Words:

and
additionally
as a result
furthermore
also
besides
likewise

Summary Words:

finally
in conclusion
lastly
in summary

Words that Order:

first
secondly
thirdly
next
when
while
before
after
lastly
subsequently

Use of Punctuation

Here's another tip: Punctuation rules help the reader understand. Applying these rules benefits both reader and writer. Your child needs to learn and use them. Remember when I mentioned that you get only one chance to communicate with your reader when writing, because you are not physically near each other? Here's what I mean.

Punctuation marks are like road signs. You've seen the one with several little ducks waddling behind their mother, or the squiggly arrow, and of course there are the changing red, yellow, and green traffic lights. These signs warn you to watch for ducks crossing the road, to slow down for a twisty road, and to stop, get ready to stop, or to go. Road signs inform you and give you important clues to help you understand driving conditions. They communicate.

Similarly, punctuation helps the writer communicate his ideas, telling the reader when to pause at a comma or to stop at a period that ends the writer's thought. Comprehension improves because a question mark should tell the reader that the writer is raising his "voice" inflection at the end of the thought; a period signals a lowered inflection. Quotation marks alert the reader to words spoken by a character in a story or by someone who is being quoted by the writer.

In the words of Edgar Allan Poe, "The writer who neglects punctuation, or mispunctuates, is liable to be misunderstood."

Jan,

Honor Roll!!

Thank you for all you have done to make it happen.

Jim

Chapter Six

Math/Multiplication

IF I COULD KNOW ONLY ONE THING ABOUT *MATH,* IT WOULD BE . . . *MULTIPLICATION.*

Why? Because this knowledge makes it easier to understand long division, fractions, decimals, square roots, algebra, and other math concepts. For example, multiplication is used for figuring the common denominators for fractions or when simplifying square roots and fractions.

It'll take only a few minutes a day for your child to learn what he needs to know, to "get it." And, you'll be as excited as he is.

Let's start by setting aside something your child *doesn't* need—the common grid of single digit multiplication facts. (Figure 6.1) Many children find it busy and confusing—even intimidating— because it requires 81 numbers, most of them redundant, to answer the 81 multiplication combinations. For example, you'll see the number **24** in four places on the grid—as an answer to 3 times 8, 8 times 3, 4 times 6, and 6 times 4. See the highlighted number **24** answers on the chart below.

Basic Multiplication Facts: All single digit numbers times each of the single digit numbers.

	1	2	3	4	5	6	7	8	9
1	1	2	3	4	5	6	7	8	9
2	2	4	6	8	10	12	14	16	18
3	3	6	9	12	15	18	21	**24**	27
4	4	8	12	16	20	**24**	28	32	36
5	5	10	15	20	25	30	35	40	45
6	6	12	18	**24**	30	36	42	48	54
7	7	14	21	28	35	42	49	56	63
8	8	16	**24**	32	40	48	56	64	72
9	9	18	27	36	45	54	63	72	81

Figure 6.1

If only we could find a way to simplify this basic learning step . . . a way to let one numeral **24** answer all four (3 × 8, 8 × 3, 4 × 6, 6 × 4) questions, and then to apply that technique to answer all the other single digit multiplication combinations.

Let's leave the "If only" and go to "presto!" When your child remembers the 36 numbers in Figure 6.2, he won't need to memorize the 81 in Figure 6.1. The numbers in Figure 6.2 represent all the products of multiplying single digits. The missing numbers cannot be produced by multiplying single digits, and therefore do not need to be memorized.

"Presto" Chart

	1	2	3	4	5	6	7	8	9
10		12		14	15	16		18	
20	21			24	25		27	28	
30		32			35	36			
40		42			45			48	49
				54		56			
			63	64					
		72							
	81								

Figure 6.2

The Quicker Thirty-Sixer

Let's look at Figure 6.2 in another form. Multiply any single digit by any other single digit and the answer will be one of these 36 numbers (Figure 6.21), ending the need for the chart with 81 numbers (Figure 6.1). When viewing the Thirty-Sixer in Figure 6.2 or 6.21, we can clearly see which numbers are present and need to be remembered, since these are listed in numerical order with the unimportant numbers missing. When looking at the products in the traditional table (6.1), it is difficult to see the numbers that need to be remembered from those that can be ignored because they have simply been repeated.

The single digits:	1, 2, 3, 4, 5, 6, 7, 8, 9
The tens:	10, 12, 14, 15, 16, 18
The twenties:	20, 21, 24, 25, 27, 28
The thirties:	30, 32, 35, 36
The forties:	40, 42, 45, 48, 49
The fifties:	54, 56
The sixties:	63, 64
The seventies:	72
The eighties:	81

Figure 6.21

THE TECHNIQUE

These 36 numbers are the only answers that a student will have to learn when mastering the basic multiplication facts. This chart and a simple deck of playing cards will add fun to the memorization. You'll use only the 1 through 9 cards. (The ace is a one.)

Your child will have success more quickly if he practices the multiplication facts in the order that I have suggested in each of the following lessons. It is normal to want to introduce the facts in numerical order, but I have found that this method is not as helpful as the way in which I will present it to you. It is also important to review the facts from the previous lessons before beginning the next. Do not proceed to the next lesson until your child has mastered the multiplication facts from the prior ones. Practice and review build confidence.

Lesson 1

First, practice the doubles (2×2, 3×3, etc.) As you point to the answers on the chart, say:

9×9 is 81 . . . you'll find out soon that this is fun.
8×8 is 64 . . . shut your mouth and say no more.
7×7 is 49 . . . now you know you're doing fine.
6×6 is 36 . . . three dozen eggs, but NO chicks.
5×5 is 25 . . . you're doing great, now give me five!
4×4 is 16 . . . you can drive 'cause you're a teen.
3×3 is 9 . . . . will you be my valentine?
2×2 is 4 . . . . also when added, now THAT'S a bore.
1×1 is 1 . . . . YOU'RE DONE!

Place a single numbered playing card in front of your child.

Ask your child to multiply it by that same number.
    For example, if a 4 card is turned over, the problem would be 4×4.

Circle the answers to the doubles (1, 4, 9, 16, 25, 36, 49, 64, and 81) on a copy of The Thirty-Sixer chart.

Next ask him to point to the correct answer on the chart.

Repeat the process.
    If your child's answer is not correct, simply point to the right answer, return the card to the deck, and repeat the process by placing the next card in the deck on the table. You don't need to say anything, but as the repetitions gain success, you can let your smile assure your child that "you've got a handle on this!"

When you feel that your child understands the exercise, set the chart aside. Start flipping the cards again, but this time have him write the answers; a little shortcut that confirms his success.

This whole process should take about 10 to 15 minutes to reach the point where you can high-five your budding star pupil.

Lesson 2

Begin by reviewing Lesson 1's doubles combinations. I like to start with the doubles because students learn a range of answers, gain confidence, and learn the higher number combinations more easily. After your child can answer the doubles correctly, move on to the 9's.

On a sheet of paper write all of the 9's answers (9×1, 9×2, etc.) Space the answers so your child can easily point to them. Call it a *9's line*:

9   18   27   36   45   54   63   72   81

Point out that the digits of each answer add up to 9, even if the digits are reversed.
    Take 27, for example. Whether you add 2 plus 7 *or* 7 plus 2, the sum is 9. The same is true of the other answers.

Also the 9's answers reverse themselves.
    For example: 18, 81; 27, 72; 36, 63; 45, 54

Refer again to the *9's line*: **9, 18, 27, 36, 45, 54, 63, 72, 81.** *Notice* that there is only one *9's line* answer per decade. For example, there is only one 9's answer in the tens decade, only one in the twenties, one in the thirties, and so on. I have used this pattern in what I call the "9's back-up trick." Kids love tricks, so I'll explain it to you now.

The 9's Back-Up Trick

Let's say that the multiplication problem is 4×9. Since one of the digits is a 9, the "9's back-up trick" can be used. Have your child look at the other digit in the problem, in this case the 4, and **back up** to the number that comes right before it, the 3. That is the first digit of the answer number, 36, in Lesson 2's thirties decade. So, $4 \times 9 = 36$. Just as $5 \times 9 = 45$, because that answer is the only one from the *9's line* that's in the forties decade. Also, just to pick

56

another example at random, $7 \times 9 = 63$ because 63 is the only number from the *9's line* in the sixties decade.

This can be confusing, but only until you go over it a few times. Let's practice with the deck of cards and the *9's line*.

- Show a 9 card on the table.

- As you flip cards one by one, next to the upturned 9, ask your child to point to the answer on the *9's line*. (If the answer is incorrect, just point to the right answer and continue turning cards and asking for answers.)

- Ask your child to tell you when he is ready to begin writing the answers instead of pointing to them.

- Continue this activity for 10 to 15 minutes.

Lesson 3

Begin this time together by reviewing the doubles and the nines. You may have to give your child more practice with the first and second lesson before adding more combinations. That's okay. Repetition is an important part of learning, and drill is easy to do within the home setting.

Start with a *2's line* as you did for the 9's, and follow the steps as in Lesson 2. Begin by placing a 2 card on the table.

2   4   6   8   10   12   14   16   18

Lesson 4

Review, review, review.

When your child is ready, go on to the *5's*. Begin by placing a 5 card on the table.

5   10   15   20   25   30   35   40   45

Lesson 5 through 9

At this point you can tell your child that he's ready to direct his own learning.

Let him choose which number he'd like to multiply next . . . the seven, for example, or one of the other numbers. When a child can do the choosing, he is more willing to stay on task.

Then do the rest of the lessons one new line per practice session, always beginning with a review of the prior combinations to make sure he remembers them.

If he hasn't truly committed the prior lessons to memory, simply review until his answers are consistently correct.

This is a random sequence of the "lines."

The 7's line

| 7 | 14 | 21 | 28 | 35 | 42 | 49 | 56 | 63 |

The 4's line

| 4 | 8 | 12 | 16 | 20 | 24 | 28 | 32 | 36 |

The 6's line

| 6 | 12 | 18 | 24 | 30 | 36 | 42 | 48 | 54 |

The 3's line

| 3 | 6 | 9 | 12 | 15 | 18 | 21 | 24 | 27 |

The 8's line

| 8 | 16 | 24 | 32 | 40 | 48 | 56 | 64 | 72 |

You can add variety (and interest!) to the practice sessions in the following ways:

Lay a row of about seven cards face up on the table.
- Let your child pick another card from the deck and place it above the original row of seven.
- As you slide the card along, have him multiply and call out the answers as fast as he can.

Make a circle of about 10 to 12 cards face down on the table.
- Have your child select a card from the deck.
- Lay it face up in the middle of the circle.
- Then have him turn over the circle of cards one at a time, calling out the answers as he flips the cards.

Challenge your child to a "miss-one-and-start-over" game.
- Have him select a card from the deck, place it face up on the table, and call out the answers as you flip the other cards one by one from the deck, next to the card your child chose.
- If he misses an answer, pick up the entire deck and start over again.
- See if he can say all of the answers perfectly. When he can say all of the answers perfectly, he meets the challenge.

Play a memory game for two people at a time.
- Place the cards evenly in four or five rows.
- Have the first person turn two of the cards face up. If those two cards are the same, the first player must multiply them correctly.
- At this time the first player can remove the match from the rows and put them aside for two points.
- That same person gets an extra turn.
- If the two cards are not a match, the first player must multiply them anyway and return the cards to their face-down position so the next player can take a turn.

Each of these activities can be done in as little as 10 to 15 minutes at a sitting. You can decide if your schedule allows for longer sessions, but you can be very effective with short, concentrated activities. A deck of cards is easy to pack in a purse or in your car's glove compartment, so you can productively fill the time when you and your child are waiting for your order at a restaurant, or for big brother to finish his guitar lesson, or for any number of downtimes that occur during your busy day. In fact, Grandma, an older sibling, or the babysitter can step in for you as well.

As some of the combinations become easy for your child (maybe he's very accurate with the 5's or 2's, for example), simply remove those cards from the deck so he can work on the other combinations. This will make the time more efficient for both of you. You should notice definite progress within one month if the practice sessions occur several times a week.

How will you know when your child "gets it"?

I have included the following multiplication time test template. (Figure 6.3) The division time test template (Figure 6.4) complements the multiplication facts, so they can be practiced after the multiplication facts are learned. I ask my students to complete each test with 100% accuracy within 3 to 5 minutes on five consecutive occasions. I ask my students to write as fast as they can, allowing them to skip any combinations which don't "pop" from their memory. (Those are the combinations which require more practice.)

Each time my students take the timed test, I place a vertical mark on the paper showing them the point-value which they achieved during their last attempt. This creates a healthy competition for them. This effective technique gives my students a goal to earn **all** of the points, and they feel satisfaction when they eventually meet it!

The timed test can be used as another source for practice after the *lines* have been used. At that point your child would answer only those multiplication problems on the timed test which deal with that particular day's lesson.

THE TAKE AWAY FROM THIS TECHNIQUE:

Keep the lessons short. Be consistent.

Multiplication Timed Test

5 × 4 =	5 × 9 =	6 × 5 =	9 × 6 =	5 × 8 =	6 × 7 =	5 × 8 =	9 × 9 =	6 × 6 =
6 × 7 =	8 × 8 =	4 × 5 =	8 × 9 =	7 × 9 =	4 × 4 =	6 × 9 =	5 × 8 =	9 × 4 =
9 × 9 =	5 × 9 =	7 × 4 =	6 × 7 =	4 × 3 =	7 × 8 =	4 × 7 =	3 × 6 =	9 × 5 =
8 × 7 =	8 × 4 =	5 × 5 =	9 × 7 =	6 × 5 =	9 × 6 =	8 × 7 =	8 × 9 =	3 × 7 =
7 × 7 =	4 × 5 =	4 × 6 =	6 × 9 =	3 × 8 =	8 × 9 =	4 × 9 =	9 × 6 =	6 × 6 =
5 × 6 =	3 × 9 =	6 × 8 =	9 × 7 =	7 × 7 =	6 × 8 =	3 × 4 =	7 × 3 =	8 × 7 =
4 × 6 =	3 × 9 =	5 × 5 =	8 × 7 =	8 × 4 =	7 × 6 =	5 × 8 =	6 × 8 =	7 × 5 =
7 × 6 =	6 × 9 =	3 × 5 =	8 × 8 =	9 × 5 =	9 × 9 =	7 × 4 =	9 × 3 =	8 × 6 =
8 × 5 =	5 × 7 =	3 × 8 =	3 × 3 =	7 × 4 =	7 × 9 =	9 × 4 =	9 × 9 =	4 × 5 =

Figure 6.3

61

Division Timed Test

20 ÷ 5 =	48 ÷ 6 =	42 ÷ 6 =	36 ÷ 9 =	28 ÷ 7 =	64 ÷ 8 =	25 ÷ 5 =	54 ÷ 9 =	45 ÷ 9 =
40 ÷ 5 =	36 ÷ 6 =	36 ÷ 4 =	35 ÷ 5 =	49 ÷ 7 =	63 ÷ 9 =	28 ÷ 7 =	30 ÷ 5 =	27 ÷ 3 =
81 ÷ 9 =	40 ÷ 5 =	72 ÷ 9 =	15 ÷ 3 =	30 ÷ 5 =	24 ÷ 4 =	54 ÷ 9 =	56 ÷ 7 =	18 ÷ 3 =
64 ÷ 8 =	42 ÷ 7 =	48 ÷ 8 =	32 ÷ 8 =	27 ÷ 3 =	36 ÷ 9 =	35 ÷ 7 =	18 ÷ 6 =	24 ÷ 3 =
49 ÷ 7 =	56 ÷ 7 =	24 ÷ 6 =	27 ÷ 9 =	54 ÷ 6 =	72 ÷ 9 =	36 ÷ 9 =	54 ÷ 9 =	63 ÷ 9 =
30 ÷ 6 =	27 ÷ 3 =	12 ÷ 6 =	40 ÷ 8 =	18 ÷ 3 =	54 ÷ 9 =	24 ÷ 4 =	20 ÷ 5 =	49 ÷ 7 =
72 ÷ 8 =	54 ÷ 9 =	81 ÷ 9 =	32 ÷ 8 =	25 ÷ 5 =	56 ÷ 8 =	28 ÷ 7 =	36 ÷ 6 =	48 ÷ 8 =
45 ÷ 5 =	28 ÷ 7 =	30 ÷ 5 =	25 ÷ 5 =	42 ÷ 7 =	36 ÷ 6 =	72 ÷ 8 =	9 ÷ 3 =	40 ÷ 8 =
64 ÷ 8 =	32 ÷ 4 =	72 ÷ 9 =	63 ÷ 7 =	16 ÷ 4 =	54 ÷ 6 =	27 ÷ 3 =	12 ÷ 4 =	81 ÷ 9 =

Figure 6.4

HONORABLE MENTIONS
Other Important Skills

THE DREADED WORD/STORY PROBLEM:

Story problems may send shivers up your child's spine. Word problems not only involve math calculations; they also demand reading comprehension skills. As in other reading material, your child needs to have a purpose for reading a math problem. Here are some suggestions to help you help your child.

The goal in reading story problems is to locate the numbers. This information is easy to find when the text uses the numeric symbols like *12* or *452*. However, sometimes the numbers are spelled out, as in *three* or *twelve*. Furthermore, the problem could use words like *dozen* or *noon* to signify the number *12*. In algebra, word problems often use letters, like x or y, which become variables within the equation. ***Read to find the numbers.***

Second, your child must figure out what to *do* with the numbers that she just found. The four operations of addition, subtraction, multiplication, and division are helpful. Rarely are the words, *add, subtract, multiply*, or *divide* used outright in the problems. THAT would make things easy. Have your child search for synonyms for these operations. ***Read to find the words that tell you what to do with the numbers.***

Let me list some of those context clues now. The words in Figure 6.5 show common story problem synonyms for the given operation.

ADDITION	SUBTRACTION	MULTIPLICATION	DIVISION
sum	difference	product	quotient
together	minus	times	by
altogether	take away	factor	split
in all	decrease	of	share
plus	lose	rows	groups
total	left	groups	sets
more	more . . . than	sets	each
join	fewer . . . than	per	rows
gain	opposites	each	separate equally
increase	comparison words:		separate fairly
tax	younger, taller,		
	oldest . . .		

Figure 6.5

63

The addition list includes the context clue, *more*.
  For example, I have two pencils, and I get *more*.

The subtraction lists the words *more . . . than*. The meaning changes in this context.
  For example, a bug has six legs, a spider has eight. How many *more* legs does the spider have *than* the bug?

When opposites (in/out, up/down, tall/short) are expressed in a word problem, your child should consider the operation of subtraction.
  For example, there are one hundred children in the school. Sixty are *boys*. How many are *girls*?

The context clues that suggest the operations of addition, subtraction, multiplication, and division are often found in the text of the problem. Sometimes these clues are located in the question portion of the word problem. On many occasions my students guess that the words "how many" or "how much" give the operational clue. These phrases tend to be distractions. Have your child focus his attention on the words listed above in the chart.

Perhaps you noticed that words like *rows*, *sets*, and *groups* overlapped the multiplication and division categories. Let's take a moment to analyze the pieces of each of the operations.

ADD: $s + s = L$ small number + small number = largest answer

SUBTRACT: $L - s = s$ largest number – small number = small answer

MULTIPLY: $s \times s = L$ small number × small number = largest answer

DIVIDE: $L \div s = s$ largest number ÷ small number = small answer

Addition and subtraction are opposites.

Multiplication and division are opposites.

Multiplication is a quick way to add when all of the numbers are the same.
  For example:

  $7 + 7 + 7 + 7 + 7 = 35$ OR $7 \times 5 = 35$

Division is a quick way to subtract when all of the numbers are the same.

For example:

24 − 8 = 16
16 − 8 = 8   OR   24 ÷ 8 = 3
8 − 8 = 0

It takes three separate subtraction problems to accomplish what can be done in a single division problem.

In most story problems there are two numbers that are added, subtracted, multiplied, or divided so your child can calculate the answer. Sometimes your child can become confused when too many numbers appear in the problem. In those cases, she may need to add all of the numbers together.
For example:

Mary read 3 books, 14 magazines, 9 newspapers, and 6 Internet sites.

Maybe it is a two-step problem.
For example:

After Augie bought his computer priced at $299.00 with a 25% off coupon, he paid sales tax of 5.5%. What did he pay for his computer?

Perhaps some of the numbers are not used.
For example:

In 2010 Tony paid $89.00 for a car repair and $135.00 for some new tires. How much did Tony spend on his car in 2010?

Even though *2010* is a number, it is not used in any calculation in this story problem.

Sometimes your child may need to draw a picture or diagram to help her visualize the situation presented in the problem. Encourage her to use reasoning, and above all, have her reread the question to make sure that her final calculation really does answer the question. The answer should make sense—*common sense*.

PLACE VALUE (See Figure 6.6)

What does 1,000 mean? Can your child give you an example of 10,000? News articles talk about millions, billions, and even trillions in terms of money and debt, but does your child have any concept of what those numbers really mean?

Ask your child to give you an example of: one, ten, one hundred, one thousand, ten-thousand. Hum, is his knowledge getting fuzzy yet? My own students have tried this activity many times. Let me share some of their typical responses.

One: 1 dog.
Ten: 10 pencils.
One Hundred: 100 pennies makes a dollar.
One Thousand: 1,000 dollars buys a car—that would be a car repair in my world!
Ten Thousand: 10,000 dollars buys a car (they try that one again)—maybe a
       used car.
One Hundred Thousand: 100,000—things are getting fuzzy.
One Million: 1,000,000—sometimes total shut down!

Understanding the concept of place value is helpful for your child when he works with money, large numbers, polynomials in algebra, and the operations of addition, subtraction, multiplication, and division, to name a few. In turn, properly aligned columns benefit the understanding of place value.

Here's a technique that will help you explain place value to your child. Suggest that place value is like a row of townhouses. Each house is attached to the next, and one family lives in each house. Each house has three rooms in it, except the house to the immediate right of the decimal point, which has only two rooms. The comma (,) is placed at the shared walls to the left of the decimal point between the houses which represent the groups of three columns of place value. (987 , 654 , 321) See Figure 6.6.

Place Value Chart

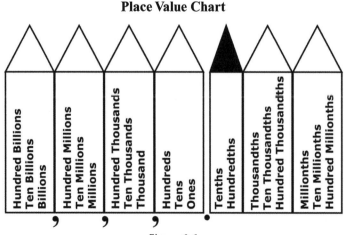

Figure 6.6

66

POSITIVE AND NEGATIVE NUMBERS

Math has a lot of RULES. There are rules for fractions, rules for decimals, rules for long division, rules for geometric proofs, rules, rules, **rules!** At least math follows its rules. I mean, take spelling rules. You know the one (*i* before *e*, except after *c*, or when sounding like *a*, as in n*ei*ghbor or w*ei*gh.) Great, they give you the spelling rule and in the same ditty, they tell you where you can't use it! Math isn't like that. Yes, there are a ton of rules, but math *follows* its rules. After your child learns them, he can apply the rules in many, many instances.

Combining positive and negative numbers is part of the process used with many other applications, so I'd like to include the rules in this Honorable Mentions section. Part of the confusion that your child may have probably involves the symbols for positive and negative (+ and −). It is unfortunate that these are the same symbols which are used for addition and subtraction. To ease the confusion, your child should recognize (+) and (−) to mean positive and negative; the words *add* and *subtract* mean the operations of addition and subtraction.

Using the Positive and Negative Chart (Figure 6.7) is easy, especially if your child asks himself: *Are the signs the same?*

Let me explain why that question will help.

When multiplying:

Multiply the numbers. If the signs are the same, the answer will be positive.

$$Ex: +7 \times +2 = +14$$
$$Ex: -7 \times -2 = +14$$
$$Ex: +7 \times -2 = -14$$
$$Ex: -7 \times +2 = -14$$

The product is always 14, but it will be positive only when the signs of the factors are the same.

When dividing:

Divide the numbers. If the signs are the same, the answer will be positive.

> Ex: +54 ÷ +6 = +9
> Ex: −54 ÷ −6 = +9
> Ex: +54 ÷ −6 = −9
> Ex: −54 ÷ +6 = −9

The quotient is always 9, but it will be positive only when the signs of the divisor and dividend are the same.

When adding or subtracting:

Have your child ask this question: *Are the signs the same?*

> Yes . . . ignore the signs for the moment while adding the numbers.

> > Ex: +10 +7 = +17
> > Ex: −10 −7 = −17

The sum is 17. Next, copy the sign of the larger numeral addend.

> No . . . ignore the signs for the moment while subtracting the numbers.

> > Ex: +10 −7 = +3
> > Ex: −10 +7 = −3

The difference is 3. Next, copy the sign of the larger numeral minuend/subtrahend.

Extra step when adding or subtracting:

This step is only needed if the problem has two signs side by side. For example, the problem might look like this: −4 + −2 or (−1) − (−8). In either case there are two signs preceding one number. THAT tends to confuse. Applying the extra step prepares the problem so the above rules for adding and subtracting can be followed.

Extra step:

Ex: −1 − (−8) . . . the −1 has only one sign before it so that numeral stays unchanged.

. . .the − (−8) has two signs before it so the extra step must apply.

Since both of the signs are the same, the 8 becomes positive. Now the problem is rewritten as: −1 + 8 and the rules for adding and subtracting can be followed.

Let me finish the problem.

$$-1 + 8 = +7$$

Ex: −1 + (+8) . . .the −1 has only one sign before it so that numeral stays unchanged.
. . .the + (+8) has two signs before it so the extra step must apply.

Since both of the signs are the same, the 8 becomes positive. Now the problem can be rewritten as: −1 + 8 and the rules for adding and subtracting can be followed.

Let me finish the problem.

$$-1 + 8 = +7$$

Ex: −1 − (+8) . . .the −1 has only one sign before it so that numeral stays unchanged.
. . .the − (+8) has two signs before it so the extra step must apply.

Since both of the signs are different, the 8 becomes negative. Now the problem is rewritten as: −1 − 8 and the rules for adding and subtracting can be followed.

Let me finish the problem.

$$-1 - 8 = -9$$

Ex: −1+ (−8) . . .the −1 has only one sign before it so that numeral stays unchanged.
. . .the + (−8) has two signs before it so the extra step must apply.

Since both of the signs are different, the 8 becomes negative. Now the problem is rewritten as: −1 − 8 and the rules for adding and subtracting can be followed.

69

Let me finish the problem.

$$-1 - 8 = -9$$

Let's take a closer look at the chart (Figure 6.7). It is separated into two columns. The extreme left hand side and middle of the chart will help your child decide the sign of the answer (positive or negative). The far right hand side will help her choose the correct mathematical operation (add, subtract, multiply, or divide). One final pointer: If there is neither a positive nor negative sign in front of a number, that number is assumed to be positive. Example: little 'ole plain 583 is assumed to be +583.

POSITIVE and NEGATIVE

	Sign of the Answer		Operation of the numbers
(Pos. Numeral × Pos. Numeral)	+7 × +2	Same signs: Ans. = Pos.	Multiply
(Neg. Numeral × Neg. Numeral)	−7 × −2	Same signs: Ans. = Pos.	Multiply
(Neg. Numeral × Pos. Numeral)	−7 × +2	Different signs: Ans. = Neg.	Multiply
(Pos. Numeral × Neg. Numeral)	+7 × −2	Different signs: Ans. = Neg.	Multiply
(Pos. Numeral ÷ Pos. Numeral)	+54 ÷ +6	Same signs: Ans. = Pos.	Divide
(Neg. Numeral ÷ Neg. Numeral)	−54 ÷ −6	Same signs: Ans. = Pos.	Divide
(Neg. Numeral ÷ Pos. Numeral)	−54 ÷ +6	Different signs: Ans. = Neg.	Divide
(Pos. Numeral ÷ Neg. Numeral)	+54 ÷ −6	Different signs: Ans. = Neg.	Divide
(Pos. Numeral), (Pos. Numeral)	+5 +2	Copy sign of larger numeral	Same signs: Add the numbers
(Neg. Numeral), (Neg. Numeral)	−5 −2	Copy sign of larger numeral	Same signs: Add the numbers
(Neg. Numeral), (Pos. Numeral)	−5 +2	Copy sign of larger numeral	Diff. Signs: Subtract the numbers
(Pos. Numeral), (Neg. Numeral)	+5 −2	Copy sign of larger numeral	Diff. signs: Subtract the numbers
EXTRA STEP: to prepare the problem for rules above			
(Pos. Sign), (Pos. Sign)	+ + 9	Same signs: Number is Pos.	Apply rules for add and subtract
(Neg. Sign), (Neg. Sign)	− − 9	Same signs: Number is Pos.	Apply rules for add and subtract
(Neg. Sign), (Pos. Sign)	− + 9	Diff. signs: Number is Neg.	Apply rules for add and subtract
(Pos. Sign), (Neg. Sign)	+ − 9	Diff. signs: Number is Neg.	Apply rules for add and subtract

Figure 6.7

DIVISIBILITY OF NUMBERS

Your child will have plenty of opportunities to use this nifty information. Divisibility of numbers will help her when she reduces fractions, estimates, simplifies roots (as in square roots and cube roots), calculates long division, and works algebraic equations—to name a few.

In the chart that follows (Figure 6.8), I have simplified the rules and given a step-by-step guide to help her through her thinking process. Single digit numbers can easily be calculated using "mental math," a term that is used to suggest that no calculator or scrap paper is necessary. Your child will feel so smart to know that she can figure her answers in her head! THAT is such a confidence-builder for students. A success or two along these lines, and you will watch your child blossom! (This technique is most useable when the multiplication tables are thoroughly understood.)

***

The top portion of Figure 6.8 (page 75) explains how the numbers on the left are divisible. For example, 2 will divide into all even numbers, and 4, 6, and 8 will divide into some even numbers without any remainder.

EXAMPLE:
Let's say your child is trying to reduce the fraction $\frac{12}{20}$.

Since both the numerator of this fraction (12) and the denominator (20) are both even numbers, the numbers 2 or 4 will divide evenly into both the top and bottom of this fraction without creating any remainder.

$$\frac{12}{20} = \frac{3}{5}$$

***

Your child can determine if 3 or 9 will successfully reduce a fraction if both the sum of the digits of the numerator, and the sum of the digits of the denominator, are each divisible by the 3 or 9. (Let me guess. You'd appreciate an example for THIS one!)

EXAMPLE:
Let's say the fraction to be reduced is $\frac{39}{87}$.

71

The digits of the numerator are added together (3 + 9 = 12).
Next add the digits of the denominator together (8 + 7 = 15).
Three will successfully divide into 12 and 15, so 3 will also divide into the
original problem 39 and 87. Go ahead . . . try it!

The number 9, however, is not worth the effort of using because 9 will not successfully divide into 12 or 15. If your child knows this, she will save time and
effort by using only the "sure thing"—in this case 3.

$$\frac{39}{87} = \frac{13}{29}$$

***

Back to the chart . . . your child will be thrilled to see that 5 will reduce any
fraction that ends in a 5 or 0, and 10 will simplify fractions ending in 0.

EXAMPLE:

The fraction is $\frac{90}{110}$.
Both 5 or 10 will reduce this fraction, but 10 will work more quickly.
90 ÷ 10 is 9 . . . the numerator is complete. 110 ÷ 10 is 11, so the reduced
fraction is $\frac{90}{110} = \frac{9}{11}$.

If your child uses the 10, she will reduce the fraction in a single step as
shown here:
$\frac{90}{110} = \frac{9}{11}$ (when reduced by 10)

If your child selects the 5 instead of the 10, she will create the need for two
steps as shown below:

$\frac{90}{110} = \frac{18}{22}$ (when reduced by 5, thus creating a new step because 18 and 22

are even numbers which are divisible by 2)

$\frac{18}{22} = \frac{9}{11}$ (when divided by 2)

***

In my four decades of tutoring, I have not discovered a usable shortcut when
dividing by 7. (Admittedly, this is not something which has caused me lack of

sleep, but I would still like to think of a trick which could be helpful.) At present I suggest that your child simply think of her multiplication 7's line. Save this calculation until last. I will discuss this during the thinking process portion of the chart.

$$\frac{49}{63} = \frac{7}{9} \text{ (when divided by 7)}$$

Eleven divides evenly into the twin double digit numbers . . . 11, 22, 33, 44, 55, 66, 77, 88, and 99. After passing 99, this shortcut fades and each number must be tested by dividing by 11.

EXAMPLE:

Let's say the fraction is $\frac{33}{77}$.

As soon as your child notices the twin double digits, she can quickly reduce this fraction to $\frac{3}{7}$. Twin double digits are easy to spot.

$$\frac{22}{55} = \frac{2}{5}$$

***

Hopefully, using the Divisibility Chart (Figure 6.8) will take some of the struggle out of those homework sessions which involve divisibility calculations. However, when your child organizes her thinking process, she can further streamline her homework exercises. She can use the information at the bottom of the chart to order her step-by-step thinking as she considers the rules that we've discussed above.

The numbers which use the most obvious shortcut should be done first. For example, it's easy to tell if the numerator and denominator are both even numbers, end in a 0 or 5, or are twin double digits. All your child has to do is *look* at them. It makes sense to do this first. Maybe the fraction can be reduced by 2, 4, 6, 8, 5, 10, or 11. If so, your child can make the calculation and go on to the next problem. If not, that leaves only the 3, 9, and 7 to be considered. How about some examples?

Ex: $\frac{14}{22}$ **=? Your child should think:**

Look for even numbers . . . YES . . . divide by 2.

Ex: $\dfrac{16}{24}$ = ?

Look for even numbers . . .YES . . . divide by 8 (faster).

. . . .

Ex: $\dfrac{44}{77}$ = ?

Look for even numbers . . . NO . . . go on.
End in 0 or 5 . . . NO . . . go on.
Twin double digits . . . YES . . . divide by 11.

. . . .

Ex: $\dfrac{21}{77}$ = ?

Look for even numbers . . . NO . . . go on.
End in 0 or 5 . . . NO . . . go on.
Twin double digits . . . NO . . . go on.
Add the digits of the numerator 21 . . . (2 + 1 = 3) . . . 3 can work, but 9 can't.
Add the digits of the denominator 77 . . . (7 +7 = 14) . . . 3 cannot be divided
  into 14 without creating a remainder . . . go on.

Try dividing by 7 . . . YES . . . she's done!

. . . .

She should continue working through each problem in this fashion. As long as she answers "no" to her questions, she should continue to the next line until she get to the bottom of the chart. If none of the numbers discussed above will reduce the fraction, she should consider dividing by a prime number.

This circumstance is rare unless her math chapter has introduced prime numbers. In that case those weird prime numbers could work.

Ex: $\dfrac{13}{39}$ = ?

Look for even number . . . NO . . . go on.
End in 0 or 5 . . . NO . . . go on.
Twin double digits . . . NO . . . go on.
Add the digits of the numerator 13 . . . (1 + 3 = 4). Stop, neither 3 nor 9 will
  evenly divide into 4.
Will 7 work . . . NO . . . go on.
Consider prime numbers . . . YES . . . divide by 13.

Primes are numbers that have no other factors except 1 and the "number" itself.

$$\frac{13}{39} = \frac{1}{3}$$

. . . .

Keep the chart in front of your child while she is doing her homework. Within a very short time, she will have committed the thinking steps to memory and she will not need the chart any longer. Another math milestone achieved!

Divisibility Chart

2	**All** even numbers
3	****add digits . . . divide by 3**
4	Some even numbers
5	**End in 0 or 5**
6	Some even numbers
7	<u>Divide by 7</u>
8	Some even numbers
9	**add digits . . . divide by 9
10	**End in 0**
11	*Double digits:11, 22, 33, 44, 55, 66, 77, 88, 99*

THINK	DIVIDE BY
1st Look for even numbers	**2**, 4, 6, 8
2nd Look for 0 or 5	**5**, 10
3rd Look for twin double digits	11
4th **Add the digits	**3**, 9
5th Divide by 7	7
6th Consider dividing with prime numbers	Ex: 13, 17, 19, 23, 29, 31, 37, 41, 43, 47, etc.

Figure 6.8

ADDITION/SUBTRACTION FACTS

Initially, your child will probably understand the concept of addition via discovering his fingers and toes. Later, playing board games will give your child practice counting, as well as adding money or the markings on the dice.

Lesson 1

I begin teaching the doubles.

$1 + 1 = 2$
$2 + 2 = 4$
$3 + 3 = 6$
$4 + 4 = 8$
$5 + 5 = 10$
$6 + 6 = 12$
$7 + 7 = 14$
$8 + 8 = 16$
$9 + 9 = 18$

Use a deck of playing cards to teach the facts as I explained in the multiplication section. Many of the same techniques can be used to teach multiplication and addition. (Please review the section regarding multiplication which was discussed earlier in this chapter.)

Lesson 2

Review the doubles.

Once my student masters the doubles, I introduce the in-betweens. (If it is easier, your child may think of these combinations as the "doubles plus one.")

In-Betweens

For example: $3 + 3 = 6$	$\mathbf{3 + 4 = 7}$	$4 + 4 = 8$
$7 + 7 = 14$	$\mathbf{7 + 8 = 15}$	$8 + 8 = 16$
$5 + 5 = 10$	$\mathbf{5 + 6 = 11}$	$6 + 6 = 12$

76

Lesson 3

Review doubles and in-betweens.

Practice using the addition time test template. (Figure 6.9, page 79)

Place ace through 9 from each suit on the table face up. Have your child select any 2 cards which add to 10. I call this activity ***Group-to-10.***

For example: an ace plus a 9 card equals 10, or a 4 card and a 6 card equals 10.

Have your child select pairs that equal 10 until all of the cards have been used.

Lesson 4

Review, review, review. Your child deserves the practice time it takes for him to succeed at getting the correct answers.

Lesson 5

Here is another back-up trick. When any single digit number is added to 9, your child can simply write one number lower than the other numeral which is not the 9 and place a one before it. *(That will need an example!)*

For example: 4 + 9 = (Back up one numeral from the 4, *which is 3,* then place a 1 before the 3. The new number is **13**.)

$4 + 9 = 13$

Another example: 6 + 9 = (Back up one numeral from the 6, *which is 5,* then place a 1 before it. The new number is **15**.)

$6 + 9 = 15$

One more time: 9 + 2 = (Back up one numeral from the 2, *which is 1,* then place a 1 in front of it. The new number is **11**.)

$9 + 2 = 11$

This is a great trick which can really give your child some speed and confidence. Here are some examples in rapid fire:

8 + 9 = **17**   9 + 7 = **16**
9 + 3 = **12**   5 + 9 = **14**
9 + 9 = **18**   1 + 9 = **10**

Lesson 6

There may be a few straggler combinations to learn. These may have to be memorized. The most likely candidates for memorization are:

6 + 8 = 14
7 + 5 = 12
5 + 8 = 13

Keep reviewing and allowing your child to practice his skills. He should be comfortable with most combinations within several weeks if you continue to practice for about 10 to 15 minutes per day.

If your child is still struggling, show him how to *count points*. The numbers **1, 2, 3,** and **4** ("pointy") are formed in such a way that your child could lightly touch his pencil—
to the top of the 1,
to the top and bottom of the 2,
to the top, middle, and bottom of the 3,
and to the exposed points of the 4.

The numbers **5, 6, 7, 8,** and **9** are too "roundy." They do not have enough angles or edges to count.

Let's say that the problem is:

6 + 3 = _____   (6 is a "roundy" number, 3 is a "pointy" number.) Have your child start with the "roundy" number by saying 6, then count the points of the other number . . . seven, eight, nine.

6 + 3 = 9.

4 + 8 = _____   (8 is a "roundy" number, 4 is a "pointy" number.) Have your child start with the "roundy" number by saying 8, then count the points on the 4. Say 8, nine, ten, eleven, twelve.

4 + 8 = 12.

After you are sure that your child knows his addition fact well, have him practice subtraction. (Figures 6.9 and 6.10)

Addition Timed Test

7 + 1 =	2 + 9 =	2 + 5 =	8 + 2 =	4 + 4 =	1 + 4 =	9 + 9 =	9 + 5 =	6 + 7 =
7 + 7 =	1 + 9 =	4 + 9 =	6 + 5 =	4 + 6 =	7 + 4 =	9 + 8 =	3 + 7 =	5 + 4 =
3 + 3 =	9 + 2 =	8 + 8 =	1 + 3 =	5 + 5 =	2 + 2 =	7 + 2 =	1 + 9 =	6 + 2 =
3 + 7 =	2 + 4 =	4 + 5 =	8 + 3 =	2 + 9 =	6 + 4 =	1 + 4 =	6 + 6 =	3 + 2 =
3 + 9 =	4 + 3 =	3 + 8 =	6 + 5 =	9 + 3 =	2 + 6 =	4 + 5 =	3 + 5 =	2 + 7 =
7 + 3 =	8 + 4 =	5 + 2 =	4 + 2 =	1 + 2 =	5 + 7 =	6 + 9 =	6 + 8 =	9 + 7 =
8 + 6 =	5 + 1 =	3 + 5 =	7 + 8 =	4 + 7 =	9 + 6 =	5 + 9 =	8 + 9 =	8 + 6 =
7 + 5 =	9 + 4 =	9 + 8 =	4 + 6 =	9 + 5 =	0 + 8 =	1 + 1 =	2 + 8 =	5 + 5 =

Figure 6.9

Subtraction Timed Test

4 − 3 =	5 − 5 =	8 − 4 =	6 − 5 =	5 − 2 =	6 − 3 =	8 − 1 =	4 − 2 =	6 − 6 =
5 − 3 =	10 − 7 =	12 − 6 =	7 − 2 =	10 − 4 =	8 − 2 =	9 − 6 =	8 − 6 =	11 − 2 =
9 − 3 =	7 − 3 =	8 − 7 =	7 − 5 =	6 − 4 =	14 − 7 =	10 − 9 =	10 − 3 =	9 − 2 =
11 − 8 =	9 − 5 =	7 − 6 =	6 − 2 =	11 − 7 =	13 − 6 =	15 − 8 =	8 − 5 =	11 − 5 =
8 − 3 =	12 − 9 =	10 − 5 =	12 − 4 =	9 − 4 =	9 − 7 =	17 − 9 =	14 − 5 =	16 − 9 =
13 − 4 =	14 − 6 =	12 − 8 =	7 − 4 =	10 − 8 =	14 − 9 =	16 − 7 =	13 − 7 =	11 − 3 =
14 − 6 =	15 − 9 =	17 − 8 =	15 − 7 =	13 − 9 =	13 − 5 =	12 − 7 =	14 − 8 =	9 − 2 =
12 − 5 =	14 − 8 =	15 − 6 =	12 − 3 =	11 − 9 =	18 − 9 =	16 − 8 =	11 − 6 =	11 − 4 =

Figure 6.10

ALGEBRA

The trick to algebra is simply placing all of the same terms together.

Example: 7a+10y+ 6k+9a-2k can be written as:

$$7a + 10y + 6k$$
$$+9a \qquad -2k$$
$$\overline{16a + 10y + 4k}$$

When adding or subtracting, the letters (16a + 10y) which are attached to the numbers can be thought of as "labels" (16 apples + 10 yams).

The above example could be rewritten as:

$$7apples + 10yams + 6kiwis$$
$$+9apples \qquad -2kiwis$$
$$\overline{16apples + 10yams + 4kiwis}$$

. . . .

The equal sign [=], greater-than sign [>], less-than sign [<], greater-than-or-equal-to sign [≥], and the less-than-or-equal-to sign [≤] separate the right and left sides of the equation, or number sentence.

Example: 3y − 7 = 13
3y − 7 > 13
3y − 7 < 13
3y − 7 ≥ 13
3y − 7 ≤ 13

. . . .

When placing the same terms together which are on different sides of the equal sign, that term must be moved using the opposite operation following the positive/negative rules discussed earlier in this chapter.

Example: 3y − 7 = 11 . . . original equation.
+ 7   +7 . . . add 7 to both the right and left sides of the equation.
3y   = 18 . . . −7 and +7 eliminate each other.

3y   = 18 . . . 3y means "3 times y".
3   3 . . . reverse multiplication by dividing the left and
right sides of the equation by 3.
y = 6 . . . stop . . . the equation has been solved.

81

When multiplying: The letters (5**a**) (3**abc**) (2**ab**), which are attached to the numbers, are added together and expressed in the exponent.

Example: (5a) (3abc) (2ab) = 30aaabbc = $30a^3b^2c$

$(-7x^2yz)(7x^2y^2z) = -49xxxxyyyzz = -49x^4y^3z^2$

$(4efg^3)(3eg) = 12e^2fg^4$ (done in single step)

. . . .

When dividing: The letters (5**a** ÷ 7**a**), which are attached to the numbers, are subtracted and expressed in the exponent.

Example: 5a ÷ 7a = 5/7 (all examples done in single step)

$-20xy ÷ 5xyz = -4z$

$14x^8 ÷ 7x^2 = 14xxxxxxxx ÷ 7xx = 2x^6$

. . . .

REMEMBER: Addition and subtraction reverse each other. Multiplication and division reverse each other.

REMEMBER: Follow the rules for positive and negative integers discussed earlier in this chapter.

REMEMBER: When working with word problems, follow the suggestions discussed earlier in this chapter.

THE NUMBER SYSTEM (See Number System Illustration, Figure 6.11)

The number system forms two large categories, REAL and IMAGINARY numbers. Real numbers have further subdivisions, but imaginary numbers are used only for negative square roots.

Real numbers separate into Rational (repeating fractions, decimals, and perfect squares) and Irrational (non-repeating fractions, decimals, and imperfect squares) groups.

Rational numbers further branch into Integers (. . . −2, −1, 0, 1, 2. . .)

Integers diverge into Whole Numbers (0, 1, 2, 3 . . .)

Natural Numbers (1, 2, 3 . . .) form the last category of the number system.

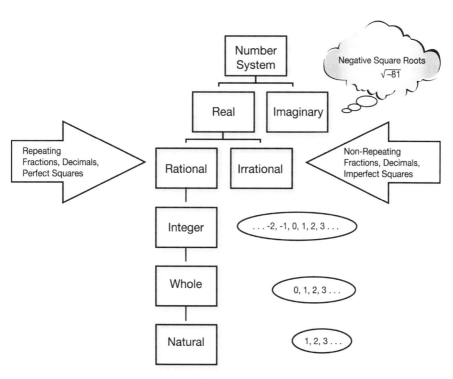

Figure 6.11

83

Dear Jan,

Just want to fill you in on how Adam is doing in high school since working with you last year. Terrific!

He loves math which is something I never thought he'd ever say! He finally knows his multiplication facts and says he uses them for math all of the time.

Thank you for all of your hard work, Jan.

Susan

Chapter Seven

Learning/Think for Myself

IF I COULD KNOW ONLY ONE THING ABOUT *LEARNING,* IT WOULD BE. . . *THINK FOR MYSELF.*

A parent's job . . . *to raise a child or to raise an adult?* If you choose the latter, you'll need to stress independent thinking and problem solving. Logic and reasoning are food for the inquiring mind. "Why" is a typical question of the developing toddler. Children want to understand how the world works and how things relate to each other. This desire to have a rational explanation seems to have no age limit. Learning involves having our world make sense.

I've learned that students have their own ways of processing information, and that thinking works better when the individual has some control. The following "do's" are important:

      1. Open your mind while I teach.

      2. Give the technique a fair trial.

After my student's consideration and trial, I encourage her to make up her own mind about using my suggestion. I ask, "Is this technique something you find usable? Help me make it clearer for you." If after my student tries the technique and likes it, I often tell her that it's my "gift" to her. If the technique is rejected, I honor her decision.

I respect my student and her point of view. Sometimes a student doesn't know the subject well enough to ask a question, and becomes confused. I need to know when the confusion arises in order to clarify the concept. A student needs to admit the confusion without worrying about embarrassment. I've tutored hundreds of students who have gradually discovered how they personally process and use information. They develop their unique ways of organizing, studying, taking notes, managing their time, and juggling the other commitments in their lives when they are encouraged to reason and to problem-solve.

Logic is the study of reasoning. Logic involves seeking the truth. In mathematics, simple tables determine the *truth value* of various sets of information. These truth tables state standard rules for judging information expressed in *simple, compound,* and *complex* sentence structures. (See Writing, Chapter 5.) Logic/reasoning can be separated into two main categories: (1) truth value—logic tables—and (2) defects in arguments, called fallacies. A fallacy is a mistaken belief based on unsound reasoning. This failure in reasoning is misleading, deceptive, and substantially weakens an argument.

Several defects in arguments hinder one's ability to reason logically. I will mention several and give some examples, but I encourage you to do independent research regarding how these defects can influence the information which your child is trying to evaluate. Among them are:

1. Going off on a tangent—*The exam should be an open book test, because it's always better when a teacher helps the students get good grades.*—Premise: A teacher helps the students get better grades. Conclusion: The exam should be an open book test.
2. Appealing to the human desire to fit in and be liked—*Cats are the most popular house pet in America, so if you get a pet, you should get a cat.*
3. Using a data set too small for the sample size—*Ryan likes Mike. Dylan likes Mike, too. Everybody is Mike's buddy.*
4. Attacking the person instead of the argument—*My teacher isn't pretty, so she can't teach me social studies.*
5. Eliciting pity—*My mother had to work late last night, so I shouldn't have to take the science test.*
6. Appealing to authority—*I read in the newspaper that some experts say that eating sugar is not harmful, so I should be allowed to eat more cake.*
7. Using stereotypes—*Princesses are young and beautiful.*
8. Over generalizing—*Popular kids don't have any problems.*
9. Using correlation instead of real cause and effect—*It is cold and rainy today. I know I'm going to get sick.*
10. Presenting a side issue or circular argument—*Premise: It is enjoyable to eat a healthy diet. Conclusion: Dieting is fun.*
11. Creating a "straw man"—*Teachers think that kids should learn the multiplication facts and they hassle kids with lots of tests. Teachers are wrong to punish like this; kids should be left alone.*
12. Using weak analogies—*Corn and poison ivy are both plants. Corn is edible, so you should be able to eat poison ivy, too.*

When developing the ability to think independently, a student needs to practice solving problems. You should encourage your child to lengthen her attention span. When your child is involved in an activity, try not to interrupt her thought process. Give her the freedom to fumble and experience failure. Allow your child the opportunity to explore her environment to the extent which time and safety permits.

As a rule, younger children need help and supervision because they have more physical and emotional needs. However, babies, toddlers, and school-aged children change very rapidly. Parents should educate themselves about child development so they can limit the amount of help they give their child as she grows and becomes more capable. It is beneficial to the child to explore her own environment. For example, parents should let their child crawl for the toy instead of outright handing it to her. It is important not to anticipate the child's every wish. Her lack of ability to communicate may frustrate her, but that will encourage the child to speak.

Providing the right amount of assistance to your child as she continues to develop her own problem-solving skills is a balancing act. The main point is to be aware that your child is making developmental strides that allow her to physically and mentally handle more responsibility. She will best learn to solve problem if she is permitted to do so. Using your parental judgment will allow her to try, perhaps fail, finally succeed, and benefit from the total experience.

"Success breeds success" is one of my personal philosophies. I've learned that when a child tastes success, she is willing to try another skill that may seem to be just out of reach. Parenting involves meeting the physical and emotional needs of their child, without stifling the child's growth towards independence. When a child struggles and succeeds, her attention span will lengthen, preparing her for other challenges.

Reasoning allows a student to find order, comprehend the truth about past events, understand cause and effect in the present, and prepare for future events. Reasoning fosters an ability to analyze, critique, draw inferences, clarify, prioritize, connect ideas, and recognize motive. Questioning develops a higher level of thinking, and is an important lifetime skill.

So how does your child learn to use logical reasoning?

Sequential ordering can begin the process. For example, ask your child to talk, step by step, about family routines. Discuss the day's activities: rising, dressing, eating, working, school, sleeping, etc. Later a child could describe the steps in baking cookies, or playing on a slide, or using an umbrella. Sequential ordering of sets of pictures is fun for children.

Another activity is prediction. Ask your younger child what to expect when the doorbell rings. An older child may be required in class to list the steps used to solve an involved story problem—a useful task in logic and reasoning.

Writing a persuasive term paper or giving detailed directions to a destination helps develop reasoning skills.

Preparing proofs in geometry, in which a reason is required for every statement made, can be a painful assignment for many students, but it is a very valuable brain training tool. Logic and reasoning require the argument to be consistent, promoting rational thinking that makes sense of the child's world.

Often, when a student understands a concept, she can process similar information very quickly. A three-year-old soon learns to remove the toothpaste tube cap before squeezing out the paste. A sixteen-year-old soon learns to look in the rear-view mirror before changing lanes. The steps usually become so automatic that they seem to have been skipped! When you encourage your child's desire to understand her world by learning to be an independent thinker, you will be raising an adult.

Jan Sixt teaches her students that learning empowers, increases self-discipline, and enhances their personal independence.

Dianne

Chapter Eight

ORGANIZATIONAL AND STUDY SKILLS/TEST-TAKING TIPS

Have you ever told your child, "Study harder?"

Study harder! Why not *study smarter?* Your child can be more productive and manage her time more wisely. Organizational and study skills are *learned behaviors.*

I teach skills in organization, study, and time management while teaching the subject material. Importantly, I encourage my students to become independent of me. At our first tutoring session, I usually announce, "your job is to dump me!" I succeed as a teacher only when my students succeed. And when they combine accuracy with speed, they gain a competence that employers look for, too. One-on-one instruction helps my students discover their own way of thinking. You can guide your child in a similar way.

When your child takes responsibility, she gains control, and that can begin at a very young age. You empower your child when you set predictable schedules for meals, play, and very important, *sleep.* You enhance organizational skills when you see to it that your child cleans up after playing and properly puts away toys and other possessions in/on designated drawers, closets, hooks, shelves, etc. Young children naturally love to sort, so the whole family will benefit when children take responsibility for categorizing and keeping their possessions orderly. Later that skill can transfer to juggling the academic workload at school.

Your child benefits when she categorizes by subjects. That means having a designated folder, notebook, or section that separates each subject. Since note-taking is important, I suggest having a different spiral notebook for each subject. Pocket folders for each subject are convenient for storing classroom handouts or completed homework. (I have tutored many students who dutifully do their homework but lose points when they can't find it to turn in the next day!)

Being organized means being able to find *what* is needed *when* it is needed.

There are many variations to the above suggestions. Whatever form your child's organization takes—folders, notebooks, partitions, loose-leaf binders—it doesn't really matter as long as she can produce what's needed on time. If she fails to do so, she must adjust and practice being organized until she succeeds.

You may have to check the folders and backpack daily for items stuffed helter-skelter, and insist that your child does this housekeeping chore. If she groans and complains, let her know that she can stop these inspections when she takes charge. She must stay organized on her own for at least one month. Also let her know that if she cannot stay organized, you'll have to resume the inspections. The policing period is difficult, but it reaps long-term benefits for both of you.

You can also encourage your child in other ways. Start with two or three good habits that you would like your child to learn. Small goals, like insisting she write her assignments in her daily planner or arrange the items that she'll take to school the next day before she goes to sleep at night, can be practiced until perfected before another skill is added to the mix. Small goals tend to increase a child's attention span and self-discipline. Children and adults see improvements differently, so be patient, consistent, and supportive as you help your child learn these organizational and time management skills.

You encourage your child to study when you (1) provide a special place to study with a table/desk, a dictionary/thesaurus, and a clock, and (2) set a regular time, maybe after a meal. Pleasure reading could take place right before bedtime. It may be necessary to limit interruptions from phone calls, text messaging, computer socialization, and television. For a period of time you may have to check homework for completeness and neatness. You also need to set a reasonable bedtime. A rested child is ready to learn.

TIME MANAGEMENT

A daily assignment notebook is a powerful time management and organizational tool. Some students may prefer using an online planning calendar that sends automatic reminders to e-mail or social media. Many school districts provide an agenda with preprinted dates and subjects in a spiral book. A scheduling calendar like this can keep your child aware of today's assignments, as well as those book reports due in three weeks. When homework is assigned, your child should write it down, and estimate how long he thinks it will take to complete. If the assignment is long term—as with a book report or project—your child should copy it in the agenda on each date until the project is due.

For example:

Date	Estimated Time	Actual Time	Assignments
Mon. Sept. 20	20 min.		Math: page 17, problems 1-25
	10 min.		English: vocab. page 14
			Science: none
	45 min.		Social Studies: Nile River project
Tues. Sept 21			So. Studies: project
Wed. Sept. 22			So. Studies: project
Thurs. Sept. 23			So. Studies: project due tomorrow

Your child reminds himself of the pending social studies project when he lists it in the agenda on each day until it's completed. This avoids the need for you to nag. If your child still can't get homework completed in a reasonable time, you'll have to step in to limit the distractions. The sooner this is done, the more successful your child can be. If he's hurrying through his homework without producing a quality product, you must insist that weekends are used for make-up work before the fun activities can begin. It should not matter to you that his teacher has already recorded a zero for that assignment. As a parent, you are trying to instill good work habits. After a while, most children will cooperate. At that point your child will be self-disciplined—an important milestone!

MANAGING CLUTTER

Managing clutter is another worthwhile skill. Just as your child will need to prioritize his responsibilities and his time, he also needs to decide what items to keep and which to toss. He'll want to keep the notes he took on World War

II last October for the mid-term exam in January. However, that practice chemistry lab the student teacher gave last October can and should be pitched. There is no need to haul around every handout and every returned homework assignment from day one. Work-in-progress is obviously to be kept. Perhaps duplicate subject folders for items kept can be filed at home in your child's desk or closet. The weekend is a great time for clearing out the clutter. Have your child turn on some tunes and start sorting!

STUDY SKILLS

Study skills and test taking skills really do take care of themselves when your child learns to take notes and make the flashcards/baby flashcards as explained in the reading and social studies chapters. The heavy lifting is easier when the daily assignments are treated seriously. Even though most teachers will not require their students to take notes, this step is truly worth the effort. Upper-elementary-level students should begin practicing note-taking while the amount of material is manageable. The reading assignments will only get longer and more involved as your child plods through middle and high school. If he is already a teenager, note-taking skills will help immediately. Start without delay.

Most of my teenage students complain that note-taking is very time consuming. If they get behind, I suggest using the weekend to catch up. They may choke back their displeasure at that idea, but they give me very positive feedback when their homework gets easier, their test scores improve, and they pick up speed as their note-taking skills improve.

Classroom teachers sometimes give their students preprinted notes. I especially see this with my younger students, but many times older students receive them, too. Such notes are usually in sentences, and represent someone else's understanding of the material. I strongly suggest that your child rework these notes into his own words because he is discovering how *he* remembers information in order to be comfortable taking tests.

Of course, note-taking works because your child wrote the note as he understood the material. Furthermore, if he wrote them only in the subject's spiral notebook, his notes are in one place. Since all of these notes are in your child's possession, he never has to wait until his paperwork has been returned to him by his teacher in order to begin reviewing for his test. He can quickly read his notes several times as his test date approaches. The night before the test, instead of rereading from the textbook, he can review the notes more purposefully. Since most of the material makes sense now, your child may need to review only the very difficult parts of the unit's content.

TEST-TAKING

There is no substitute for knowing the material. Your child will be surprised how his daily work ethic has painlessly prepared him for the exam. That point aside, he may not know an answer to a test question and need to skip it. Later, he may find a clue elsewhere on the test to help answer that skipped question. Remind your child to stay alert for such a "gift." If a question is skipped, he should clearly mark it so that he can quickly find it later.

Negatively worded questions are often easier to think about when they are stated in a positive form. Let's consider the possible answer choices to the example below as if the question had been asked, "What **is** hot?" *(The answers below correspond to the italicized question.)*

"What item is <u>not</u> hot?" *(Think of this question as reading, "What is hot?")*

a.	Recently used stove	*yes*
b.	Sun	*yes*
c.	Refrigerated lunch meat	*no*
d.	Boiling water	*yes*

Choice *c* clearly stands out as different from the other answers. Refrigerated lunch meat is not hot, which ultimately answers the original question.

....

Sometimes math answer choices can be "tried" by placing them into the equation and doing the calculation. For example:

15% of what number yields 45?

a. 290
b. 300
c. 275
d. 350

Your child can begin by plugging answer choice (a) 290 into the original equation.

15% of 290 = 43.5   no   That answer doesn't match the one needed in
                              the original equation. Try another choice.

15% of 300 = 45   yes   Stop trying. This answer works!

Choice *b* is correct.

....

True/False questions are usually false when the words *always, never, none, no, every, all,* or other words of totality are written in the statement.

....

Another test-taking technique is the *brain dump*. Let's say that your child needs to remember the formulas for area and perimeter of geometric shapes. Perhaps he must use several definitions or be able to list the order of the scientific method.

Example of *brain dump*: Triangle............. a = 1/2bh.............. p = a + b + c
                         Square...............a = bh................. p = 4s
                         Rectangle...........a = bh................. p = 2b + 2h

After memorizing the above information, he should not begin taking the test until he writes down the formulas, or definitions, or scientific method (*brain dump*) in the margin of the test itself in case he needs it later. This lessens the pressure so your child can proceed with answering the questions. He may never actually use the information that he brain dumped, but it is there if he does.

....

Should your child guess at the answers if he is not sure? That depends upon whether there is a penalty for guessing. As this book goes to print, the SAT (Scholastic Aptitude Test) for college entrance subtracts one-quarter point for every incorrect answer. On the other hand, the ACT (American College Test) does not penalize for an incorrect response. Encourage your child to ask his teacher if incorrect answers (or incorrect spelling, for that matter) will be penalized.

Writing test questions is an art form. Sometimes context clues in the question hint at the answer. Your child should not hesitate to ask a teacher for clarification of the test question. He shouldn't lose points because he misunderstood the question.

Teachers want their students to understand and succeed. If your child disagrees with the way his test answer was scored, he should respectfully question his teacher. He may have to explain why he answered as he did. There is a human element regarding test making and test taking. Constructive feedback can benefit both teacher and student. Encourage your child to speak up for himself. Some lessons extend beyond the classroom and are grooming the student for other life situations.

EXCUSES

From time to time, the twists and turns of life will get in the way of your child's time management and organizational skills. This is exactly why it's important to budget time and to prioritize responsibilities. As your child develops, he will be able to handle a more complicated workload, keep track of more intricate details, and respond to longer tests without undue stress.

However, some of you may be dealing with a child who is argumentative or uses excuses to avoid doing what he is supposed to do when he is supposed to do it. At this point, I usually explain to my student what constitutes a *good excuse*. Here's a tip: *Most of my students love to be thought of as older than they actually are, and they like to have some input about what happens in their lives.*

From my experience, *a child equates aging with gaining power.* Older children typically enjoy more freedom, are scrutinized by their parent less frequently, and have more privileges. Parents who tend to be protective need to be convinced that their child will not self-destruct when he gains more freedom. (I mean, who in their right mind, would hand over the car keys to a 2000-pound-weapon-on-wheels without some level of trust?!)

Your child needs to understand that trust comes from doing what he says he'll do. He needs to walk the talk. If a child cannot meet his current commitments, he is giving up his power. He is performing at a maturity level below his chronological age. He is actually practicing staying a kid.

So . . . when a child doesn't meet his responsibilities, what constitutes a good excuse? In my judgment, good excuses basically fall into two categories:

I Had a Life Crisis

- Death/birth—of a family member, a close friend, neighbor, pet
- Accident—of a family member, a close friend, pet, self
- Illness—of a family member, a close friend, pet, self
- Unexpected event— a storm occurred or perhaps Aunt Becky, Uncle Jim, and their children stopped in for dinner and stayed too long afterwards.

Thankfully, life crisis events don't occur often. They can be very disruptive and are not caused by the child. *I had a life crisis* is a good excuse!

I Didn't Understand

"I didn't understand" excuses come from a teacher's failure to explain the lesson well. This is not the child's fault. However, he should be encouraged to find an alternate source of information to help him understand the concepts. Perhaps the library, the Internet, etc. could be helpful. Independent study is a student's ultimate tool toward independence.

An unacceptable use of the *"I didn't understand"* excuse is when a teacher does explain the lesson well, but the student waits too long to do the assignment and now can't remember what the teacher taught. The use of this excuse doesn't fly, but is a valuable reminder to budget time for the homework for newly taught material as soon after the instruction as possible.

The prolonged use of other excuses simply keeps your child at an immature level. Meeting his deadlines is a sure way to gain freedom, enjoy less parental oversight, and receive more privileges—in other words, **gain power**.

Dear Jan,

My son is so much better prepared for school thanks to your assistance and guidance. He is successfully using his agenda. There is less stress in our home, and more structure!

Thanks again,
Beth

Chapter Nine

When Will I *EVER* Need THIS?

A nose-scrunching child complains, "When will I *ever* need *this*?" I admit that when I was a student, I often pondered the same question. Now it's obvious to me that the academic disciplines intertwine to the benefit of the student.

The longer I teach, the clearer it becomes to me that academic subjects have much in common. For example, teaching English sentence structure helps me explain word problems in math. The punctuation within the sentence very often groups the numbers or enhances the relationship between the numbers in the math problem. I use the concept of place value in math in order to explain scientific notation in chemistry. Teaching about the elements of the short story helps me explain some concepts in social studies, and helps students write their book reports.

As a parent, you can help your child understand that she shuts the door on her opportunities each time she decides that learning a particular skill will *never* serve her. The fact is that none of us can know the future. (I was shocked to realize that I had a *book* to write!) Life can be surprising! *You* probably have some wonderful surprises yet to come in life, too. Your child's life is a blank slate with so many possibilities . . . if she is prepared.

The basic skills of language, thinking, reasoning, organization, time management, writing, and mathematical calculation are like the basic food ingredients. They can combine in different proportions to make many recipes. The concepts of math, for example, have many applications. Here are a variety of real life situations that may occur in your child's life which would use math concepts. (The numbers have been excluded intentionally.)

1. **Travel**—Thuy wants to compare the cost of flying or driving to her business conference.
2. **Personal Finance**—How much will Jean owe over the course of her loan if she borrows the money to buy this furniture?
3. **Health**—Marc is dieting. He needs to compute the amount of nutrients that he needs as his weight changes.
4. **Business**—Robert wants to compute his employee deductions so he

receives the largest sum of money with each paycheck while also meeting his tax obligations.

5. **Sports**—Nate is relocating. His pool table is half as wide as it is long. What is the smallest room size it will fit in? (Remember: Nate still must have room around the table to play the game!)
6. **Cycling**—Melissa is planning a long distance bike trip. She wants to pedal at a steady rate of speed.
7. **Crafts**—Grammy wants to know the cost of knitting an afghan using yarn of two different kinds and prices.

The combinations are endless.

Help your child understand that these basic disciplines give her the flexibility to take advantage of the most possibilities to support herself and meet her life's potential.

"What are you going to be when you grow up?" Many of my younger students readily answer this question, but as students enter the high school years, they're not so sure. Most of them may have an idea about the career they *don't* want to explore, but few clearly see their paths. Their struggles with math, reading, science, or social studies have influenced their thoughts.

So to the complaint, "When will I ever need *this*?"

I answer:

"What job will you get to support yourself? How long will it last? Most people change jobs several times during their lives.

List the challenges you may face as you get older . . . sickness, accident, marriage, children, divorce, natural disaster, job loss, war, moving, death of a loved one. I don't know what your challenges will be, but, for sure, challenges will happen.

If you really decide not to learn this subject well, as least consider against shutting down so completely that you spoil your overall grade point average. Then remember your distaste for this subject when you think about your college major. Choose something that doesn't waste your time or money.

When I was younger, I remember thinking, 'When will I ever need *this*?' Now, I know.

Afterword

Most animal species nurture their young for several months to several years before they reach adulthood. The human animal has the unique opportunity to observe this growth and enhance its offspring's life for nearly two decades.

As a private tutor, I feel privileged to fulfill part of this role and to know its satisfactions as I watch a child's development from dependency to dependability, from helplessness to confidence, from cluelessness to a young adult with ideas, insights, and improved ability to reason and communicate.

About the Author

Since 1971, I've taught children and adults, most subjects, and all grade levels, as well as college courses—including foreign exchange students, adults learning English as their second language, and students unable to attend school due to illness, surgeries, emotional problems, or pregnancies. Teaching via private instruction became very satisfying. I decided that I had found my niche.

Moving around the country with my military husband during his assignments, I taught in Alaska, Washington, and Montana, finally settling in New York. Years later I returned to my native Ohio to help care for my aging parent. Some of my experience was gained while teaching in a traditional classroom; most was not. Recently, I also began teaching via the Internet.

I have coordinated lesson plans for parents who home-school their children, and I have conducted the instruction for a tutorial program offered by the UAW at the Ford plant in Avon Lake, Ohio, for workers' children. I've prepared students for various examinations, including SAT (Scholastic Aptitude Test), PSAT (Preliminary version of the SAT), ACT (American College Test), GRE (Graduate Record Exam), GED (General Educational Development), OGT (Ohio Graduation Test), OAA (Ohio Achievement Assessment), TOEFL (Test of English as a Foreign Language), PRAXIS (practical application of learning, an examination for teaching certification), Catholic High School Entrance Exam, the New York State Regents Exam, the Pipe Fitter's Licensing Exam, and Broker's Licensing Exam.

I teach skills in organization, study, time management, and efficiency while I am teaching the subject material; and—importantly—I encourage my students to become independent from me.

I have been the guest speaker at various PTA/PTO meetings. In 2007, I was inducted into Who's Who Among America's Teachers.

After more than four decades of teaching a variety of subjects to hundreds of students, I still find that one-on-one is stimulating and productive, for both the student and for me—in my case, even well past my formative years.

I love what I do!

Jan Sixt

List of Charts

Index

reason, 33-35, 47, 49, 85-86
reasoning, 30, 65, 85-88
relationship, 20, 33, 35
resolution, 27
responsibility, 87, 89
reverse, 47, 56, 81-82
reword, 34-35
root, 14
S
Scholastic Aptitude Test (SAT), 94
science, 37
Scrooge, 28-29
self-discipline, 90-91
semicolon, 46
sentence structure—
  complex, 43, 47-49, 86
  compound, 43, 46, 48-49, 86
  simple, 43, 45, 48-49, 86
sequential order, 87-88
setting, 25-26, 30-31
shortcut, 71-75
sign—
  equal, 81
  greater-than, 81
  greater-than-or-equal-to, 81
  less-than, 81
  less-than-or-equal-to, 81
  of the answer, 67-70
silent letter, 12-13, 16-17
social studies, 37-40
sort, 89
spelling, 11-17
static, 28
story element, 25-33
story problem (see word problem)
straw man, 86
subheading, 34
subject, 20-23, 43-47
subtraction, 63-65, 67-70, 79-80, 82
success, 40, 87
suffix, 14-16
supervision, 87
syllable, 13
symbol, 35, 67
T
technique, 9, 16-17, 23-24, 31-33, 35, 37-40,
  43, 55-60, 66, 71, 76, 85, 94
television, 90
test-taking, 93-95
theme, 25, 29

time management, 90-91, 95
timed test template—
  addition, 79
  division, 62
  multiplication, 61
  subtraction, 80
toddler, 85, 87
transitional words—
  cause/effect, 50
  contrast, 50
  order, 51
  summary, 50
  support, 50
true/false, 33, 37, 94
truth table, 86
U
unit, 34
V
variable, 63
variety, 59
verb, 19-24, 43-47
vocabulary, 23-24, 37-40
vowel, 13-14, 16-17
W
whole number, 83
word problem, 63-65, 82
work-in-progress, 40, 92
writing, 43-51